Soulmate

or

Cell Mate

Also by Jackie Woods

Books

Spiritual Energy Cycles

Journey to Ultimate Spirituality: Advanced Teachings & Workbook for the Modern Seeker

Audio Titles

Abundance

Anger Management

Chakras

Dream Interpretation

Energetic Parenting

Meditations and Needs

New Business Paradigm

The Power of Real Choice

4 -Way Mental Communication & Emotional Sharing

In addition, selected Interactive Workshops by Jackie Woods are available on CD.

Please visit **www.jackiewoods.org** to begin your journey towards empowering your Heart for extraordinary living.

Soulmate

or

Cell Mate

You Make the Choice

A Guide to Healthy Relationships

BY

JACKIE WOODS

Adawehi Press
P.O. Box 1549
Columbus, NC 28722
www.jackiewoods.org

ISBN 1-933690-00-3

Printed in the United States of America

Library of Congress Control Number: 2005934871

To my son Russell,
for a lifetime of support.
I am forever grateful.

Contents

Preface

As the consciousness of humankind advances, so must the role of relationship. To interact with others the same way you did five years ago means that your relationship skills have not been given an opportunity to keep up with an evolving you. In counseling with couples, I have repeatedly witnessed the relationships as being substandard to the quality of the individuals involved.

The purpose of this book is to give you tools that will help eliminate the gap between your personal awareness and your relationship skills. While many of the examples given refer to couples who are intimately involved, the content applies to all on-going interactions. It is my belief that relationships are a great tool in helping people realize their full potential.

In bringing unconditional love
into your relationship,
you get to have
more positives than negatives
by creating more real than unreal.

Soulmate
or
Cell Mate

1

Does perfection exist? There isn't a person alive who has not at least occasionally fantasized about how a perfect partner would treat them. Some people really believe that relationship perfection can happen if they become either perfect or find the perfect match. On the other extreme, many people believe that even mediocre relationships can exist only in fantasies. So what is the truth about relationships? Do you find a Soulmate, develop one, or just settle for a Cell Mate?

Well, the chance of finding someone who matches all of your fantasies exactly is almost non-existent, but with some careful changes to your definition of what makes a relationship good and maybe a little better understanding of how relationships work, then you can definitely move away from Cell Mate and move towards Soulmate. The trick is that you get to choose which parts of each person become food for the relationship. You may need to be a little flexible on the containers these "ingredients" come in. Let's begin by looking at how we select those "ingredients."

Of course everybody's picture of perfection is different, but it seems there are a few traits that make everyone's list. At the top of most lists is unconditional love. The definition varies from person to person, but the essence of its meaning goes something like this:

- Unconditional love means that "flaws" are accepted and dealt with in a kind way.
- It means that the good, heartful qualities are allowed the freedom to express in forms that fit them best.
- And finally, a definition of unconditional love includes acknowledgement of the ways each person shows love.

Acceptable "Flaws"

No two people love in the same way. Some people shower their lovers with compliments, while others cook meals or fix cars to show their Love. In other words, people love by giving what they know how to give. This is not a measure of the totality of their Love, but merely a chosen way to share it. This doesn't mean, however, that their concept of unconditional love can't stretch beyond their favorite way of sharing Love.

In fact, you will be able to find many relationship prospects who will agree with the three stated points of unconditional love. But problems always seem to arise when it comes time for that definition to be put into practice. At first, your flaws and theirs are overlooked because you are having such a wonderful time exploring each other's potential. Alas, when the honeymoon period is over and the potential hasn't materialized (but the flaws have), then unconditional love flees to the place of unrealized potential.

Generally, the land of misfit potential and misfit love contains a lot of anger and judgment. It is a nasty place that poisons everyone who enters. It is bad enough for one person in a relationship to enter this land of misfit potential and misfit love, but it is even more unfortunate when that person pulls the other half of the relationship in also. Once this happens, the title "Cell Mate Relationship" starts forming over your heads.

I'm sure you won't willingly go to the misfit place of anger and judgment, but suppose you accidentally end up there. What then? This could be a sign from "the powers that be" that you need to condense your very thick book of fantasies so you have room to add a few pages on how to look more kindly on the other person's flaws.

You might also add an addendum to your unconditional love definition that puts the unrealized potential vs. good qualities in proper balance. It might read something like this: "Good qualities must exceed the fantasy potential — even if it means giving up some of my fantasies."

FORMS THAT FIT

In order to truly realize this new goal, where good qualities outnumber fantasies, you must become cognizant of the forms good qualities express through. It would also be wise to include a statement that covers how many flaws you can tolerate, and of course, you must make certain that the flaw list does not exceed the good qualities list. These added intents to your unconditional love definition certainly will mean you have taken several steps away from Cell Mate and are definitely headed in the direction of Soulmate.

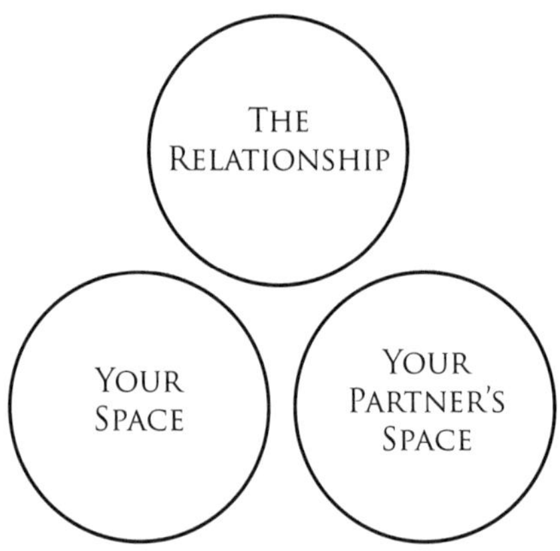

If you can picture a relationship as a third entity, it will be easier to understand how a relationship can become a Soulmate relationship. Hold in your mind a picture of three circles (as above). One represents your space, one your partner's, and one the relationship. Into the individual spaces you can place all the virtues and faults of each respective person. This means the third circle, or relationship space, is an empty canvas. The two of you can decide together that only good things get to go into it. Consequently, you don't have to be perfect people in order to have a Soulmate relationship.

Cell Mate relationships are also three circles. The only difference is that they are defined by misconceptions formed from past programming. For example, one detour from happiness to the place of Cell Mate relationship is taken when you decide to transform your partner into your perception of perfection. When the forms that your partner's qualities are expressed through are not on your acceptable list, the tendency is to imagine that they could be, with just a little help. In fact, if your partner doesn't accept your help to become "perfect," then you will probably make those unacceptable forms proof that your partner doesn't love you.

Rather than go through all the pain of feeling rejected and unloved because you can't change your partner, wouldn't it be much easier to negotiate some forms that would work for both of you? This may mean tweaking your acceptable qualities list as well as your acceptable forms.

For this negotiation of forms to work, the person with the "unacceptable" form must recognize that the form is not their expression — it is just a vehicle for expression. If they feel the form is who they are, they will feel judged. For example, one person may choose to express Nurturing by cuddling in front of the television. However, if television is boring to the Nurturing recipient, then that is not a good relationship form for Nurturing. The television watcher must recognize why he or she feels nurtured when they get to cuddle while watching their favorite program. They must then find another form in order for that flavor of Nurturing to express in the relationship circle. The new form, of course, must be something that works for both partners.

Most people have a credit balance on the good side of the expressive forms ledger, but their choice of how they want to use those credits may not match the form needs of the other person. While few people set out to be seen as total slobs or inconsiderate brutes, they oftentimes end up being seen that way. For instance, a good hearted person may be awkward in social situations. That person's manners may not match the viewer's standard for manners. However, he or she still can be social on the tennis court, where the form expected is not interactive etiquette but physical skill.

Even if your qualities and forms are a good match for one person, they may not be for another. For example, in trying to be considerate, a detail-oriented person might keep his or her partner informed as to what is going on by talking about every single detail of the day during the evening meal. If the partner is a "get-to-the-bottom-line" type of person, all those details would be seen as a selfish hogging of the conversation. (Not to mention how boring it would be!) This detailed expression of Communication and Consideration might work with someone else, but here, there is a mismatched form.

Changes in the forms are an inevitable necessity. However, it doesn't work to have one person making all the changes. It usually works best for a couple to find a form that doesn't lean to one side or the other on their preference lists. This doesn't mean that a person can't choose to express in one of his or her partner's preferred forms, but it must be a good fit for both people. Choosing forms just to please others builds resentment in the end.

For this plan of choosing forms that fit you (and also work for the other person) to be profitable, you have to get to know *who you are as heart energies* (such as Nurturing, Consideration, Creativity, Trust, Honor, Play, etc. — several are listed at the end of the book) rather than forms. Then, and only then, will you be willing to give up old forms of expression in order for the relationship to move towards Soulmate. Change has to be a desired thing. Redoing your habits is too difficult a task to accomplish without wanting to do it. Your partner can support you in change, but never can a partner do it for you.

Let's say your partner has agreed to give up the silent emotional role and start acknowledging his or her feelings openly. You are thrilled! Of course you want to offer your heart energy of Support, but your old form must go because it will no longer fit. Your old form of support was to feel everything vicariously *for* your partner. For instance, when someone would treat your partner badly, he or she would be silent while you got angry. Since you can no longer "do it for your partner," how are you going to bring Support? One way would be to ask how he or she felt about what happened. Another would be not to dominate the emotional relationship space with your feelings. Tell your journal your feelings if you need to, but don't overwhelm your partner, who's just beginning.

Many forms can be discovered that will fit the bill for both of you. However, forms must continually change for your relationship to grow. The tendency in most relationships is to find something that works and then, no matter what happens, externally or internally, hang on to it. Change for the sake of change is not good, but change for the sake of growth is a neccessity.

Nothing will kill your spirits faster than a stagnant relationship. Are you afraid that change will be for the worse instead of the better? If so, you are not alone. In fact, I have had people say to me that they were afraid to grow personally because they would outgrow their relationship. It was clear to me in every single instance that the relationship had only a limited survival time. Even if the two stayed together, the relationship would die without growth, and eventually the Spirit of each person would grow dim.

Relationship growth can be unsettling. Yet, at the same time, it can be extremely exciting. It means that not only will you get to bring new heart energies into the relationship circle, but you also will get to grow up the ones that already exist.

To grow existing heart energies, you might choose to bring more Understanding and Sharing to your present Communication.

You might also allow more time together to support you in growing up Trust a bit more. Certainly growing Trust and expanding Communication are exciting, but no two people respond the same way to growth, thus giving the unsettled feeling that an unknown doorway is about to be entered. A new relationship is being forged!

Relationship growth happens only when both of you are open to growing individually. If you are both growing at the same pace and growing up the same energies, then relationship growth doesn't feel so unsettling. However, that is seldom the case. Even if you and your partner are growing the same heart energies at the same pace, each of you won't respond to the lessons in the same way. The trick is to see entering each new phase as an adventure.

It seems to be a universal truth that people want to hand hard-earned lessons on a silver platter to people they love. If one half of a couple gets on a healthy eating kick because the awareness of the heart energy of Health is growing in them, then they automatically want their other half to experience it too — whether the other half wants it or not. More than likely, they will proclaim the importance and benefits of healthy eating at every opportunity. However, if the partner isn't ready for that lesson on Health, then the profundity of the other person's information will fall on deaf ears and, more than likely, tension will thicken.

Another example: Your job has forced you to bring more Organization into your awareness and you discover it is a helpful heart energy. You go home and attempt to bring Organization with you by suggesting that your partner make the bed and clean the dishes every morning. Oops! The silver platter syndrome is trying to force itself into the picture. Your partner has not acquired any new Organization and sees no reason why it should be part of the relationship. The gift of Organization offered on your silver platter of advice goes unappreciated.

This imbalance may cause things to feel uneasy for awhile, but if you go back to the "agreeing-on-forms-together" plan, the no-organization person may start to grow that energy. Instead of cleaning the dishes and making the bed, you may both agree to pick up your things before going to bed. In the Health example, you and your partner might agree to stop going out to eat at places that serve greasy, non-healthy food. By agreeing on forms together, you can each have a bigger share of Organization and Health. Naturally, new forms will need to be added as these energies grow in the relationship, but you have to have a starting place.

Are you beginning to see that change doesn't happen by manipulating or nagging? Change happens by continually choosing forms together — forms that fit the new energies that you both wish to include in the third circle. Flaws are no longer seen as troublesome things to be eradicated. Instead, they are the small spaces you can grow from. When the emphasis is on the real heart energies, and those are played up by agreeing on forms that fit, flaws seem inconsequential. Your acceptance list is now becoming greater than the flaws you believed you had to tolerate.

Acknowledging Love

This brings us to the final item in our unconditional love list: Everyone wants to have their Love acknowledged. Perhaps even more than being loved, we want our Love to be acceptable. I'm not sure which would come in first in a race, but both deserve to be winners. Luckily, both being loved and having our Love received can be experienced when heart energies and forms are both taken into consideration.

People tend to act in very loving ways, not really knowing what energies are contributing to the Love they are sharing. For instance, some mothers are super careful about protecting their children from danger because Safety is one of the contributing energies of their Love. Other mothers bring Affection in large measure. Some wrap their children in Understanding. While still others bring little of Safety, Affection or Understanding, but Support their children with their homework and school activities 100 percent.

It is usually from your mother's offerings of Love that you develop your offerings. Some of your Love energies may be quite similar to your mother's, while you may have developed others simply because you missed them in your mother's offering. To pick and choose is your right, but to deny yourself and others the right of choice is to court disappointment.

Discover what heart energies fall under your umbrella of Love and be open to other people's Love umbrellas being different colors. Keep in mind that even the same colors can come in different shades. You may both bring the energy of Loyalty, but one of you may define it as not having sex with anyone else while the other may expand the definition to cover not even looking at anybody else.

While recognizing different qualities of Love is vitally important to a relationship, it isn't always easy to do. What happens if one of you has a Love energy that the other doesn't even see as important? If bringing Abundance home in the form of money is important to your partner and it is no big deal to you, what will happen? Discounting the gift your partner brings is not a good idea. However, you can acknowledge the energy gift of Abundance carried through the money without getting all caught up in the form of having things. In other words, the heart energy behind the form needs to be the appreciated item. It is possible to receive Love in forms other than yours only when the energy given is the subject.

Needless to say, all the traits on your perfect partner list have not been discussed, but unconditional love makes up for a wide array of them. You don't really need to discard the totality of your perfect partner list if you can deal effectively with that first item: unconditional love. For in bringing unconditional love into your relationship, you get to have more positives than negatives by creating more real than unreal.

You may still fantasize about how it might be if your partner looked like your favorite movie star or how nice it would be if your honey noticed your new outfit. But even if you're an expert at fantasizing, everything pales in comparison to having your flaws dealt with in a kind way, having the freedom to express your best energies, and having your special Love energies acknowledged.

You are well on your way to a Soulmate relationship when you and your partner are willing to work together to define a third space from the real heart energies that you each bring. However, to do that you have to learn how to communicate.

*Interactive communication means
that each person not only receives
the communication on the level it is given,
but also gives back from that same level.*

The Big Picture of Communication

2

Talking is most often associated with the word communication. While talking can be a tool for communication, it is only a small part of the picture. In order for talking even to be classified as communication, there must be energetic interaction. It is the energy exchange that happens in an interactive situation that engages real communication.

I am sure you have encountered big-time talkers who never interact energetically. They talk at you instead of with you. Usually people who talk but don't communicate have only one form of sharing. Some people can only recite textbooks. Others tease and joke. Still others can only share themselves by doing for you. Oh yes, and there are always the "Moaning Myrtles" somewhere in the vicinity.

Broadening Your Communication

If you limit communication to any one part of you — physical, emotional, mental, or spiritual — your energy is not flowing through you. There is no vertical movement of energy, only horizontal. Think about it. If you believe communication is talking about one area of your life (i.e.,the way you perceive life best), how much communication is going to happen? Probably not a lot. In fact, you may not even know there is a world beyond your familiar form of perception.

Unfortunately, some of your relationships may have fallen by the wayside simply because the way you perceived and communicated about life was so different from that of your partner's that interaction just didn't happen. For that to change, both you and your new partner must expand your picture of perception to cover the other person's way of perceiving. Even if you just expand to cover two of the big four-part picture (physical, emotional, mental and spiritual), communication within your relationship will improve. The greater the number of the four parts that you and your partner share, the greater will be the energetic flow between you.

When you and your partner talk from the same perceptions, you at least have a communicative interaction in small measure. Generally, this is classified as a good relationship because you both "speak the same language." The limitation is that you will never give each other reason to broaden your horizons. Living without all four of your parts activated is like choosing to be handicapped.

Imagine a relationship where no feelings are exchanged. Does that conjure up images of the strictly mental Spock character on Star Trek? Just as limiting would be a relationship where the only subjects discussed were feeling ones. In this mostly "emotional reality," the good is really good but the bad is really bad. Then, of course, you have seen couples who seemed to function from fantasy land. They have no practical plans or budgets, but they hold on to their belief that it is all going to work out in the end. Some couples love to do physical activities together such as working in the yard, watching television together, perhaps even taking trips together, but they don't ever exchange ideas, feelings or fantasies. Once again, the small picture may seem okay from the inside, but step back and you can see how much is missing.

If you want more than a small measure of interactive communication, then you need to become aware of yourself as a whole person. Simply stated, you will need to start perceiving the world through all of your parts – physical, emotional, mental and spiritual. Expanded self-perception is the first step to greater communication with others. Once that self expansion takes place, you will be ready to take step two. This is the interactive step.

Interactive communication means that each person not only receives the communication on the level it is given, but also gives back from that same level. This doesn't mean that you let your partner share about his or her life and then you share about your life. Interactive communication requires sharing each offering as if it were a beautiful gem. When you have something to offer from your life that enhances the gem, then that should be shared. The temptation is to take turns bringing separate gems. This type of sharing is not interactive communication. Take, for example, a wife who communicates her Love by doing things for her husband while her husband is content just feeling the Love they share and doesn't see a need for doing or words. Are they really interacting? Of course not, but if the wife acknowledges her husband's silent gift by patting his hand, and the husband obviously relishes his wife's cooked Love offering, then they are at least interacting in a limited way — through the physical. This is certainly better than no exchange. However, if each partner added one or more parts to the interacting, the relationship space could be much bigger.

Even when you exchange from all four parts of you, you will still probably have one favorite. If that doesn't happen to be the same favorite expression vehicle as your partner's, you will need other outlets. Without adding to your expression résumé, you will probably become bored, dissatisfied, or even restless. You may then start looking at the relationship as the problem when it isn't.

For example, you might need to have a "sharing buddy" who is only a telephone call away if your strongest communication perception is the feeling world. While that is a perfectly wonderful perception, a partner who perceives the world logically is not going to want a heavy dose of feeling interaction on a regular basis. This is not to say that your partner is off the hook just because you have found someone or something else as your expression outlet. It only means there doesn't need to be a fight for dominance between the physical, emotional and mental perceivers. Imbalance of any kind in a relationship spells trouble. So keep your interactive communication in balance by finding other outlets where they are needed.

The Four Types of Communication Perceivers

Communication can go way beyond words, but words are still handy for verifying what interactive exchange has happened. Thus, you need to expand your thinking vocabulary to thoughts that come from your partner's land of perception. Since there are four basic parts to every single person, then it stands to reason there are four basic thinking vocabularies. Naturally, there are words that are unique to each individual; however, each of the four perception areas (physical, emotional, mental and spiritual) has its own thinking vocabulary.

How a person experiences life most intensely is how that person's mind takes in perceptions. The physical perceiver talks about doing because his or her mind sees those images. The sensations that the emotional perceiver picks up and tries to translate into words are the feelings of the situation. The mental perceiver's mind is always trying to understand, so it will pose thought puzzles to be put together. The spiritual perceiver's mind will always be searching for new possibilities to expand the current situation.

The people who experience life by understanding it are the mental perceivers. They ask a lot of questions and want explanations about everything. They usually like to read, do well in school, and love to have the right answer. They can't imagine doing something just for the sake of doing. There needs to be a reason for the doing. Nor can they conceive of just sitting in silence for long periods of time to enjoy the exchange of a particular heart energy such as Love. Violent emotions make no sense in their understanding, so emotions often take a back seat to these folks. This is the box they must expand from in order to interact more fully.

The people who experience life through their feelings don't really care if it makes sense in the same way the mental perceiver does. To the emotional perceiver, if it feels good, it is important and thus makes sense. If it feels bad, it is to be healed. These people are the ones you go to when something exciting has happened. They know how to interact with you in that experience. In fact, most emotional perceivers can interact with the whole spectrum of feelings from excitement to grief. Their gift to the feeling world is great, but as is true with each type of perceiver, they are limited in interactive communication unless they are willing to go beyond their field of perception.

Physical perceivers believe most of the other three thinkers to be either lazy or inept because they fumble in the physical world so often. These physical thinkers often prefer doing to words. In fact, their word vocabulary is usually short and to the point so they can get back to doing. Having a spiritual thinker around to add possibilities at the beginning of a task is oftentimes helpful, but once the physicals are engaged in the task, their focus becomes very singular. They don't mind making mistakes as much as the emotional thinker, who would feel bad because of the mistake. Making a mistake to physical perceivers only means they need to do it different.

The spiritual perceivers hate being pinned down to one idea. They are the ones who enjoy the freedom of flitting from one possibility to another. Exploration is their gift to the world. However, they may prove to be difficult to drag along at a fast thinking pace because they'll believe too much is being missed. They don't want to go directly from the problem to a solution. They want to explore several solutions so there is always a choice. It may seem as if they are slow in coming to a decision, but in reality, they just cover more ground before they make a decision. Spiritual perceivers actually can enjoy interacting with all three of the other thinkers as long as they don't have to be limited to the other person's "small" space. They thrive on seeing the big picture. Please don't confuse spiritual perceivers with spirituality. However, it is often the big picture of spiritual thinking that opens people up to spirituality.

Once you identify your own style, the plot thickens as you try to figure out how to have interactive communication with all these "alien thinkers." You will never be them, but you can expand to cover and include your other non-favorite parts by beginning to develop a vocabulary for each.

Think of it this way:

- Those with physical preferences are the structure builders; therefore, their words bring physical reality to a conversation.
- Those with a feeling preference add color and design.
- The details are taken care of by the mental perceivers.
- The spiritual expanders keep conversations from becoming too tight and boring.

Always keep in mind that interactive communication goes beyond words. The way you perceive life will most definitely affect your thinking and use of words, but it doesn't stop there. Regard the touch of a physical perceiver to be just as much an offer for exchange as the well-worded speech of a mental perceiver. Hold the passionate support of an emotional perceiver to be as valuable as the spiritual perceiver's new vision of how to make your harried schedules work together. In receiving the shared gifts of others and giving yours in return, energy gets exchanged, and the interactions are fulfilling.

Becoming an interactive communicator is going to uncover inner parts of yourself that have been safely tucked away. The strong, more confident parts of you may be excited to finally get to step forward and have a voice. However, once you reach the place inside where your wounded inner-child lives (and where your shy, scared child hides) you may need to put outer communication on hold for a short time while you attend to your inner child. By stopping to attend to your inner fears and insecurities, it becomes possible for you to proceed with your communication lesson from a stronger space.

Once you have a healthy parent
for your inner child,
you are then ready
to put some serious thought into
what really constitutes your personal space.

Parenting *your* Inner Child

3

Everyone has an inner child. Your inner child most likely has some endearing ways and some not so endearing ways of relating in the grown-up world. How you were responded to as a child and how your needs were attended to will determine how that (now internal) child interacts in your life today. Many of the childlike physical, emotional or mental conclusions you came to as a child are still being acted out by that child in your adult life. Some of these child-written notes stored in your present memory bank say that your needs can't be met by your "parents," so the child has to get them met the best way a small child can. For your inner child in your present grown-up world, "parents" might mean all adults who play an important role in your life.

When a child's needs are met by the parent, then the child begins to develop an inner parent, i.e., the adult. However, if a child's needs aren't met, then the child has no parent role model for those needs and, as an adult, tries to meet those needs in childlike ways. Do you have an inner parent? If not, don't despair. You are grown-up now and can learn how to parent a child. You can learn interactive communication with your inner child just as you can learn it with other people.

Not to learn interactive communication with your inner child is to orphan parts of it. So what happens to grown people who still have a predominance of orphaned parts? Most grown-ups who seemingly function well in the world have simply learned to hide or ignore their inner child (especially during work hours). However, the inner child hidden away in the emotional closet with a mental lock on the door still has to be fed.

You may have an inner child who is docile and lifeless, or you may have a rebellious little demon that kicks at the door constantly. Either way, your child deserves a healthy parent.

Childhood Behaviors

Some children learn to get their way by throwing a temper tantrum. They find that if they yell, cry, or pout long enough, at least one parent will give in and let them have their way. While that is not too attractive, even for a small child, it is really unbecoming for your inner child to act out in one of those ways in your adult life. Even though it isn't really fair, we usually save those behaviors for our closest relationships. After all, doesn't our child need to have a say somewhere, sometime?

Some children learn to play one parent against the other or push both parents' "buttons" at once. For instance, a child might go so far as to get sick in order to get the attention of both parents. It works if the parents are programmed mainly to take care of the problems in life. Weak parents can be manipulated, while indifferent parents tend to just let kids fend for themselves.

Over-protective parents will program their children to have far too much fear about life. Critical, demanding parents will cause their children to have poor self images. Caring parents, who are determined to give their children much more attention than they themselves got growing up, can end up turning their children into selfish monsters. So where is the healthy zone?

Energy Needs of the Inner Child

The healthy zone is found when you can listen to the need behind the behavior. What is your inner child asking for when he or she wants to buy things at the store that you don't really need. Is it Acknowledgement, Power, Love, Beauty, Worth? If you can discover the real energy need, then you can redirect your inner child to different forms of behavior. This means that you won't become a victim of your programming, nor will you try to tuck it away.

This method of discovering the real need behind the inappropriate behavior can be of use in dealing with the inner children of others as well as your own. Believe me, inappropriate childish behavior exists in all your relationships. In fact, you may like your best friend because your inner kid acts out in the same way your friend's does. This works fine if you keep your relationships limited to one area, but when you start expanding to include all four parts of the other person and all four parts of you, then the kid stuff will need to be addressed.

Let's say you work in an office with a gossip monger. Obviously, this person has a need for worth. Why else would they need to make someone seem less than they? Probably there was a critical parent somewhere in this person's background. How can you bring worth to that person without sounding patronizing? First of all, you will need to observe where your co-worker brings real parts of himself or herself. You won't need to lavish praise because, more than likely, that person will be able to receive only a small portion anyway. However, you can let your co-worker know you value the realness expressed — while at the same time expressing your position on the unreal. You might say, "I appreciate how much Persistence you have in maintaining quality in our office, even though I don't always agree with the way you go about it." At the same time you are acknowledging what is real in the person's offering, you must be careful not to encourage or support their misbehaving child.

Now let's look at your inner child. How do you behave when you don't get your way? Do you pout, punish, rant and rave, withdraw, or go do what you need to make sure you get your way all by yourself? To use the technique of addressing the real need with your child, you must first loosen your grip on whatever outcome you are attached to having. Only then will you be able to find a need hidden quietly behind the nasty behavior. The need will be the heart energy behind the form. Your second step will be giving that need a new behavior pattern.

What happens when you forge ahead with all your old patterns in place and don't stop to evaluate? To answer that, let's look at one example. Let's say a partner or a friend has promised to go to a movie with you and at the last minute the person backs out. What would you do? You were really looking forward to putting work away for awhile and getting to play a little. Needless to say, you are disappointed, maybe even angry. You may decide to go anyway, but you still can't forgive your friend for letting you down. You go and even enjoy the movie, but it wasn't as much fun as it could have been. In other words, you felt your need for play got whittled down to a smaller size because your friend didn't go with you.

Had you stopped to consciously recognize your need was the heart energy of Play, you could have released the form of going to a movie with a friend. You could have had more choices around forms and perhaps found a better fit. You could have asked your next door neighbor over for a game of cards. Perhaps you could have gone to the mall and tried on very expensive clothes. The possibilities get multiplied once the energy is the theme.

In seeing the shape of the real energy need beyond the form, you can eliminate the disappointment that comes from not quite getting there. This kind of healthy parenting makes you a better relationship partner, by decreasing your dependency on another to meet your needs. You also make it easier to live with yourself!

It is often easier just to blame someone else than acknowledge your responsibility to parent your inner child. In fact, I have found that this unhealthy blaming method rates as a top problem in most relationships. There is definitely a close correlation between the overuse of blaming and all the unhealthy marriages and co-dependent friendships out there. Even though it is a big problem, there is a simple solution — inner child parenting.

Listening to the real needs of your inner child also will awaken you to the delights of seeing life through the eyes of a child. You then can begin to bring back the Wonder and Adventure of your toddler. You can reconnect with the Expectancy and Curiosity of your teenager, and you will be able to embrace life with the Fullness and Simplicity that all healthy children exhibit.

You may handle your inner child in different ways, but your child can only be healthy when you take on the responsibility of being a good parent. You are already parenting, even if it is not in a healthy way. Unhealthy parenting requires more effort than healthy parenting because you have clean-up duty. You have to mend broken relationships and make excuses for your child's embarrassing behavior. And yes, by doing these cleanups, you are supporting your child's bad behavior.

Ask yourself repeatedly, "What is my real need?" In your interactions ask, "What is their real need behind their words or behavior?" By asking those questions, you are allowing your adult to take a healthy parenting stand. Your adult now has the information needed to guide and support your own inner child and to interact with others' inner children if necessary.

Once you have a healthy parent for your inner child, you are then ready to put some serious thought into what really constitutes your personal space. How much of it are you ready to share in a relationship space? Healing inner parts takes time, and those fragile pieces of your space need to be protected. What people so often yearn for is to have someone else love and parent their inner children. Definitely, you want a partner who is sensitive to your inner child, but the healing can only come from you.

You won't have to wait until all parts of you are healed and ready for a relationship. Remember, a relationship has a space of its own. You get to define what it will look like. Share as little or as much as you want. The other person's needs do not determine what you give. You must look to see what expressions of yourself you are ready to share. Then, and only then, are you ready to work with someone to create a healthy relationship space.

A relationship exists
when the heart energies
that make up the essence
of each of you
get to interact.

Your Space • Their Space Our Space

4

When you begin to discover the difference between real energy needs and forms, you will begin to see clearly that your partner has a space and you have a space. No longer will the forms be the solution to the needs in your relationship. Instead, each of you — in your individual spaces — will handle your own needs with real energies, while the relationship will only deal with shared expressions of those real energies.

Movies, books and even best friends emphasize that the whole reason to have a relationship is so that your pseudo-needs will be met. However, think about it. Even when you get your "emotional way" or you get to be "right," are you really sharing a space equally? Couples cry for equality and balance while clinging to the fiction that relationships exist only to take care of each other's physical, emotional or mental needs. The need of your spiritual self to express energies that have defined themselves from your Heart, more often than not, gets left out. It's no wonder so few relationships make it.

Real Energy Needs

You must dig down to the energy that you need to express, find a form that fits it, and then express yourself into that form in order to exist in time and space. If your forms aren't filled with real energies, meaning your energies aren't filling forms that fit, then you have no space. You don't really exist. Without a personal space, you certainly won't be able to create a relationship space. It takes two people to create a child as a third entity. A relationship third entity is no different.

Since your partner also must have a space before a relationship can be created, what happens if he or she won't get past the "take care of my needs" phase? What if your partner is stuck in his/her attachment to a particular form? What if he/she has never dealt with their inner child? In other words, what if your partner isn't acknowledging his or her own space?

The answer to all those "what ifs" is that you must try to see past the behavior your partner is presenting to the real energy need and support him or her in going there. Of course, you cannot make your partner hunt for his or her own space nor can you heal your partner's wounds, but you can point the way.

This must be done out of caring for the other's realness, not out of wanting the person to act real. There is a big difference. One has attachment to an outcome, the other doesn't.

Stay cognizant of the fact that there can be no connecting or resonating in an unreal space. If your partner isn't offering you a real space and has no interest in finding one, then don't get pulled into the morass. Back away quickly and wait for their light to dawn. By withdrawing some of your energies from the relationship — the ones that have no exchange — you are free to offer your energies where exchange is possible. This may mean finding a hobby, a pet, a friend, or a worthwhile cause.

Pulling away from the situation can also be a solution when the other person badly wants things done a particular way, wants to find the "one right answer," or wants you to carry their life's burdens — and they want — and they want — and they want.

Instead of backing off, you may decide to try to guide your partner to an awareness of the real need behind his or her desires. Be careful, this can be dangerous! There is danger in that you can easily abandon your inner child to take care of your partner's.

There is also the danger of taking on the bad habit of manipulation. Even seemingly well-intended suggestions can be disguised manipulations when you strongly want your partner to change. The only way you can support your partner in awakening to his or her unrealness is by not caring how your gift of Support is received. Then it is simply an expression from and for your space — not for the relationship.

Wants are un-owned needs. Demands are wants that have decided to go to war. Demands from others have to be handled more carefully than wants. In those cases, you may just choose to say, "That idea doesn't work for me right now," and change the subject. There is little hope of negotiation while demands are on the table. Since demands are a stronger version of wants, they need a firmer parenting stand.

Falsely believing you are supporting the relationship, you might find yourself giving in to your partner's fixation on how and why things should be a certain way. When you try to make your partner emotionally happy, peace may happen on the surface, but down deep you will feel empty. The energy connection that makes your relationship thrive won't be happening.

What you are really looking for is that closeness that comes from the sharing or resonating of realness. Those kinds of energy connections join you and your partner in a sacred space. It is those moments you keep trying to recreate. Neither control nor subservience is a satisfying substitution.

If your goal is to build a third space, a relationship space, you will have to find what is real for your partner and for you. Then, and only then, can you come to an agreement on what will work for both of you. Manipulating or demanding change will only create a pseudo-relationship. Giving in or giving up won't create a real relationship either. The "our" space of shared realness is the end result of two healthy adults choosing to resonate their Hearts together.

Having an "our" space requires vigilance and cooperation from both parties. While it is indeed an asset for two people to be endowed with their own spaces, it does not guarantee a relationship. You can respect others, enjoy them, be attracted to them, and even love them, and still not have a relationship. You can be honoring of their space and feel that they greatly appreciate yours without sharing an "our" space. Coming to a common ground with ideas, sharing feeling experiences, and supporting each other in physical tasks all add to the comfort in being together. However, none of those compensate for the desire of two people to create a third space. Just as two people can have sex and not have a baby, two people can live and do things together and not have a relationship space.

A relationship exists when the heart energies that make up the essence of each of you get to interact. Those energies, such as Commitment, Play, Humor, Loyalty, Compassion, Persistence, Order, Communication, etc., come from the core of your being. They are energies that take different shapes and sizes in each of you. For example, you may have a lot of Awareness and Listening shaping your Support, while your partner may have the heart energies of Persistence and Determination defining his or her Support. It is this variety that gives you your uniqueness, and it is also this variety that can keep you and your partner separate if you don't learn how to find ways for your diverse energies to fit together.

A good fit is not about compromise or taking turns in getting your way. Instead, it is about being open to new and different ways of expressing who the two of you are together. This means you must see yourself separate from your individual expression forms. Forms for expressing your essence are just containers. They are not what you have to share. They are not who you are. They are only the exchange vehicles.

Bringing two people into relationship around the energy of Health might look like this: One partner loves bicycling and begs the other partner to join in. The other partner does try, but finds bicycling to be much too strenuous. Bicycling is not Health. It is a form for expressing Health. Since the form doesn't work for both, they must decide on another form for expressing Health together. The non-bicyclist may decide to jump on a trampoline while his or her partner is bicycling. Does this work for sharing energies? As a matter of fact, it does. Energy is not limited by time and space. It is shared by intent. Being in relationship doesn't mean you have to do everything together!

Forms of expression are necessary and add the final touch to a beautifully combined mixture of energies, but forms are not the reason a relationship exists. You wouldn't think of serving a meal with beautiful but empty dishes. Even though you might enjoy the beauty of the well-arranged table, your stomach wouldn't feel very satisfied. Relationships experience that same lack of satisfaction when they concentrate on just the external forms rather than what goes into those forms.

There are three spaces that must exist in any of your relationship situations: your space, their space, and our space. Each space contains energies defined by forms. And, of course, the "our" space is a creation from each of your individual spaces, but it cannot contain the totality of the two. Thus, the "our" space can never be bigger than the lowest common denominator of your individual spaces. If either of you neglect your own personal space, even if it is for the sake of the relationship space, you both will soon have little to offer. When your individual space shrinks from neglect, all of your offerings will be small. How can you give generously to a relationship if you have little to give?

Relationship Balance

If you find yourself to be the lowest common denominator in some of the joint gifts offered to the relationship — that's fine. To be the lowest common denominator in all heart gifts offered to the relationship means you need to find a partner with smaller heart energies so you can have more balance. Balance must be maintained in the amounts given as well as between the three spaces: yours, mine and ours. Imagine one of the personal spaces being huge and the other personal space being tiny. What possibility of having a balanced relationship does this couple have?

As I said, a relationship space cannot be more than the lowest common denominator because people can't bring more than what they have to bring. While intimate relationships work best when each person's total space is close to the same size, small, balanced relationships are certainly possible in other circumstances. A friendship might even be smaller than the smallest individual space, depending on how much is brought to the relationship. You don't need to bring all of you to all of your relationships. However, we sometimes imagine more is being brought than is really so.

A great deal of honesty is required to keep relationships balanced. When honesty is absent, the bigger of the two people may try to put more energy into the relationship to make it fit his or her image of what the relationship should look like. The smaller person may try to contribute more forms to make the energy seem bigger than it is. It would be the answer to many of your relationship problems if these solutions for the imbalance of personal spaces worked, but unfortunately, they do not. Instead, not accepting imbalance usually makes one of you feel inadequate and the other resentful. Being honest about what you are really getting from or giving to a relationship is a better approach.

It is rare to find two people perfectly matched in every energy size. Even if you find you are perfectly matched in the beginning, hopefully you both won't stay the same size forever. For it is when both of you are growing and maturing in who you are as energy beings that the relationship will grow as well. However, growth also means that the balance between the three spaces will change often. Thus, adjusting to new energies and redefining new forms must be seen as life-giving exercises, not a death sentence.

If you or your loved one views change as death (rather than life), growth will be a scary thing. Growth then will be seen as something to avoid if you want a lasting relationship. Obviously, this is not the answer. Instead, you must embrace constant fluctuation and readjustment in your relationship spaces. If you are afraid to grow personally for fear your relationship will change, what will be the outcome of your relationship? The verdict is not a pretty one because no one person can remain constant. Not even the third entity, "our" space, can stay the same. Each space is maintained by energy, and energy is always moving. The only other alternative is to have empty, dead spaces — spaces devoid of energy because they are not fed.

Let's assume your choice is a vital life rather than a living death. That means you choose movement, and you are accepting your purpose for being alive. After all, aren't you really just a composite of heart energies taking form into shapes that can express into the physical? Because you are made up of energies, and energy must move, your purpose in life must be to move. Simply put, that means you flow into your personal space through all of your parts: physical, emotional, mental, and spiritual. You then are able to flow energetically from your space into relationship spaces. Your shared interactions in these relationship spaces then come back to you to keep the flow going. Welcome to the world of the living!

Your essence was created for the purpose of expressing, and each time it expresses, it grows and matures. Have you ever had the opportunity to watch a child develop? Children will keep trying something until it is learned. Then they move on to master the next set of forms, all the while growing up inside. The purpose of any relationship is to let you express in order to grow up your inside parts. Relationships are not supposed to be an end unto themselves.

Letting your relationship serve the growth of your personal space so that your personal space can, in return, serve the growth of the relationship should be everyone's goal. This perspective puts all three spaces — yours, theirs and ours — in perfect order and balance. This means you have to stop looking at the size to measure value and look instead at the rate of flow. For example, you may be bigger than your partner in Creativity, but your partner may be expressing a bigger percentage of his or her Creative energy into forms. Which person then brings more value to the relationship? Naturally, it is the one with the most expression. A reservoir serves no one unless it is allowed to flow.

Using every relationship, not just your intimate one, as flow stations takes the pressure off needing to be seen as perfect by others. You are no longer trying to measure up or make things turn out right. It means you no longer need others to give you Love, Power or Wisdom. Instead, your value now comes from the movement of your energies of Love, Power and Wisdom into life for interaction and back again to fill you. This new value system implies that you need relationships with others only in order for both people to flow.

Are you willing to go there?

Relationships can enhance
your reason for being alive by
creating bigger Flow spaces,
but beware — they can also block Flow
if they remain cluttered.

Keeping Relationship Spaces Clear

5

Since it takes defined heart energies from "your" space and "their" space to make an "our" space, and it is necessary to have relationship spaces in order to have the life generating substance of flow, it becomes essential to keep all of your spaces clear. Naturally, you can't make other people do internal house-cleaning, but you can confront their negative energy clutter when it affects your relationship space. Keep in mind that their clutter can never affect you directly because you only deal with others through the third entity, "our" space.

Clutter and "Bothers"

This is a tough concept to grasp. I am sure there have been many times when it felt like others were hurting you personally with their clutter of negativity. They were only hurting you if you didn't redefine the relationship to exclude their petty reactions or selfish demands. There is no reason to be anyone's victim. Others can never hurt you if you take responsibility for adjusting your connection to the "our" space in order to stay in alignment with what is really being brought. In other words, you get hurt when you let others' negativity come into the relationship space. You don't get hurt when others' judgments, manipulations or reactions are seen as just that — *their* judgements, manipulations or reactions.

By keeping the container that your combined energies flow through pure, either person in a relationship can have a bad day or go through a rough time, and the relationship will stay intact. Think back to the earlier example of telling the demanding person, whose demand was disguised as a suggestion, that you didn't want to participate. You were avoiding having the relationship hit by falling negative energy debris. The demander can not hurt you or the relationship space unless you allow it.

Besides the big obvious negative clutters that need to be kept out of the relationship, there are the little "bothers" that you often find too embarrassing to share. These little "bothers" are the equivalent of dust balls in your house. A few may not be noticeable, but when they accumulate and are scattered around, they not only look bad, but are unhealthy as well. Clutter comes in all sizes and all of it must be swept away.

For example, instead of berating yourself for being irritated that your partner doesn't load the dishwasher in the right way or put away those little stacks of paper that he or she leaves lying around, state your irritation. But don't state it for the purpose of having your partner change to alleviate your frustration. State it to start the clearing process in your space. Just getting something off your chest will make you feel better, but it won't change the irritating form. You must clear the upset and replace it with a new definition of a form that fits you, even if it is only for you and not the relationship.

For instance, you might share that it bothers you that your partner doesn't have as much Order as you, but don't stop there! If your partner wants to work with you to bring into the relationship definition forms that support Order, that is wonderful. But you are not left wanting if that isn't the case. You can still define, for you, that you are going to put all your partner's stacks of "stuff" in one location. Remember, if both people don't agree to a change, then you must do it for yourself. You can still empower expression in your own space without anyone's participation.

It doesn't mean the other person is unloving if he or she won't erase the problem for you by agreeing to a new form. It just means the other person is choosing, in that moment, not to be in relationship. That does not mean that person doesn't want to be in a relationship with you. I repeat, it only means that at that time, and concerning that heart energy, the person either doesn't choose to be in relationship or can't give as much as you are asking.

Let's say you are living with someone who never shuts the closet door, or consistently forgets to turn off lights when he or she leaves, or rarely washes his or her own dishes when a meal is finished. You have asked him or her to complete these tasks to no avail. In the absence of cooperation from your partner, you start doing these things for him or her. But of course, a little resentment builds each time. Naturally, you assume the resentment is there because the other person is acting like a stubborn, inconsiderate, selfish partner.

Instead of taking this worn-out path of thinking, let's look at another option. What if you were to clear your space of frustration for the purpose of letting more of your Completion energy express? This would be much more productive than trying to change your partner. In actuality, you already have what you are asking for or the absence of it wouldn't bother you. If your partner either doesn't have the energy of Completion in his or her essence storehouse or doesn't choose to express it in the way you want, then you aren't left bankrupt. You can use these opportunities to express Completion yourself by shutting the door or cleaning the dishes "for yourself." Don't stay stuck in the "It must get done." Instead, stay in the "It must be expressed."

Once you realize that the energy is the subject rather than the form, you will become a lot less dependent and needy. Keep in mind that if you can recognize the need as a particular energy to be present (such as Completion), it means you have that energy within you. People can't see what they don't have. If you can see it, you can give it. You are giving to the one who wanted it — you! Now your space is not only clear of resentment but is growing your energy of Completion even bigger.

Clearing your space is your responsibility because it benefits you. It does more than just make you feel better or make your life easier. Clearing your space actually creates a space for that energy substance we are calling "the real you" to have a place to exist. You are more than you were before, so in a way, your partner gave to you by not giving to the relationship.

The need to have other people do it "the way you want" is one of the main culprits in the destruction of healthy relationships. You understand, of course, that if your partner has to meet your needy standards, then you have to meet your partner's also. As you can see, the spotlight soon gets focused on the forms of doing. This either means giving in, or an all-out power struggle. In fact, even the people who give in will usually try for power in a passive/aggressive way. As you can easily see, a once clear relationship space can become a cluttered mess in a short time when neediness is the focus.

This unhealthy way of relating has never proven successful. It beats me why people keep using it. Maybe no one ever showed them a better way. Or perhaps the incorrect belief that a relationship is the source of Love (as well as all other heart energies) is so strong that it overpowers the real reason for having a relationship — Flow. Yes, a relationship space is a great opportunity to have more heart energies flowing from you and to you, but that doesn't mean the relationship is the creator of those energies.

You may fare better with several smaller relationships, or one big one may be the answer. Either way, you can trust that the author of your being (or Higher Self) will create the exact number and sizes of relationships that you need. The amount of Flow you need is the answer.

Relaxing and letting your Heart create what and who you need will certainly take a lot of pressure off your primary relationship. The essential core of your being then can be in charge of shaping the energies you need to express at any given moment. The relationship will no longer be the sustainer of your life. The Flow force in you is powerful. Trust it, and your need for control and perfection in forms will disappear. Relationships will be transformed into clutter-free channels for Flow.

Clearing your Personal Space

It is neither possible nor wise to ignore all the irritating things your partner does. But it is possible and wise to clear your feelings about those things so you can get to the energy you need. Certainly, you should ask your partner to share with you the energy you want so you can include that in your relationship space, but you can't make your partner do it. After all, it may only be your need, not theirs. You will find relationship contentment once you learn to take care of your own needs and celebrate the ones that can be shared.

Once you are comfortable clearing your personal space, it will become easier to clear the relationship space as well — even when your partner is not willing to participate. Clearing the relationship space with the help of a partner may be more satisfying, but it is really no different from doing it alone. Your upsets need to come out in either case. However, you must be careful not to blame your partner for the upset or the unwillingness to bring more. Your emotion is simply there to remind you that it is time to add a form to your personal space that will give the heart energy behind the upset an outlet.

Even when both of you are willing participants, frustration builds when one of the forms the two of you have chosen to express through no longer works. This is simply a clue that it is time to re-evaluate and re-define. Approach the supposed "problem" with anticipation and excitement about the new growth it will bring to your relationship. To not grow means death. So celebrate the opportunity to grow!

However, clearing frustration is not the same as dumping your frustration. Dumping happens when there is no intent to get to the energy behind the misfit or absent form. Bringing the problem out into the open can feel freeing, but it won't last if you don't go further. After you clear the emotion it will be much easier to see what energy was absent.

After you both have shared the emotional part of yourselves, cleared your relationship space of clutter, and discovered the energy that was needed, you are ready to select a new form. Double check to see what raw material you have to work with, and don't get caught up in perfecting the form. It may take a bit of trial and error to find a new form, but that is just part of the adventure.

You can count on your physical, emotional or mental voices to tell you when they are not content, but don't let them control you! They are just red flags to tell you there is a problem. If you let any or all of them take over, the task of clearing becomes much more difficult. Your Heart essence wants Flow. All the other three parts (physical, mental and emotional) want solutions. However, if you clear the clutter from the other three parts, they will give up their bias for solutions and give in to the sheer pleasure of having a new heart energy flow through them.

The only difference between clearing by yourself and clearing with your partner is that you get to have help and the end result will be a bigger Flow. After all, two Flows are bigger than one! Relationships can enhance your reason for being alive by creating bigger Flow spaces, but beware — they can also block Flow if they remain cluttered.

Both strengths
and weaknesses
must be seen as gifts.

Strengths and Weaknesses

6

It takes a clear space in order to value your strengths and your partner's strengths. It is difficult to see what is good when you are in the middle of an emotional or mental whirlwind. At those times, the glass looks half empty instead of half full. Nor is it easy to be forgiving of faults when you are in a negative whirlwind. Therefore it behooves you to clear your personal space before entertaining the relationship space in any way. To overlook the strengths brought to a relationship, or to be unforgiving of faults, leaves little of value in the third entity relationship space.

Everyone has strengths and everyone has weaknesses. That's a "what is" of life. The difficulty lies in supporting strengths in the other person that you don't have in yourself. The first hurdle is seeing and acknowledging them as beautiful, valuable gifts without feeling deficient about yourself. The second hurdle is when you are ready and willing to let the other person's strengths grace the relationship, but you are clueless as to how you can support something in which you have had no experience.

Let me put in a warning before we go on. The strengths that benefit a relationship are not the same as the ones the world often puts on a pedestal. For instance, having an education is considered a personal strength by the academic world. To have money is considered an important strength by many class-conscious people. A pretty face counts high on the strengths scoreboard in Hollywood. Relationship strengths, however, are products of a well-developed character.

The energies that make up any person's character belong uniquely to that person. Most people have the energy of Love as part of their character, but it will never be exactly the same in any two people. One person may emphasize the energy of Loyalty through Love, while another may take the energy of Sharing beyond the norm. If these two people don't acknowledge Loyalty and Sharing as strengths towards defining a relationship Love space, problems may arise.

To continue this example, imagine how insulted the Loyalty ones would be by the Sharing persons' insistence that the Loyalty ones tell them everything. "After all," think the Loyalty ones, "don't they know I would never do anything to hurt them? Why are they so distrusting?" While the Sharing ones think, "If they really love me, they would want to share their world with me." In this scenario, the gifts of Loyalty and Sharing as aspects of Love just got thrown into the wastebasket.

Finding Center Point

Even though it is now obvious that the strengths of each person's character must be given a space of honor in the relationship, there must be a center point. That point is precisely halfway between acknowledging an energy to over-indulging it. An energy becomes a relationship strength when it steps beyond being recognized to being expressed. It does little good to have an energy if there is no form to bring it into physical existence. However, letting it express to the exclusion of other energies turns it into a weakness.

Let's say you are a very compassionate person. Indeed, Compassion is a wonderful energy to possess and one most relationship partners welcome. Yet to overuse it by trying to help any and all of your friends would probably cause the expression of such things as Completion in your job and Devotion to your family to be excluded. This exclusion of other heart energies for the sake of one would turn that strength into a weakness.

Let's bring that example even closer to home. If you give your partner an overdose of your Compassion, or any other heart energy, you will dishonor the relationship space by not allowing your partner to contribute. Nor will you be honoring your partner's personal space when you deny him or her the opportunity to grow an energy. Any time a person is strong in a certain area, it is easy to confuse Love with over-giving. It is never a loving act to take away a person's opportunity to grow. Not only is it harmful to your partner and the relationship to over-indulge a heart energy to the exclusion of others, but it is harmful to you as well. In fact, this kind of over-indulgence will not only cover up your strengths, it will hide your weaknesses.

I knew a couple who had been married sixty years. The husband was a quick decision maker with a lot of good common sense. No fault there. However, he made all of his decisions, all of his wife's decisions, and all of the relationship decisions. Not good! When he died, the wife was left helpless in the area of decision making. Had he brought his decision making strength into the relationship in a balanced way, it would have supported the weaker half that his wife brought. She would have had the opportunity and space to develop and become stronger in her own decision making. Instead, her space was covered up by his spillover in the relationship.

Relationships should provide a safe place for you to grow up your energies. Unfortunately, weak energies are considered to be one and the same as weaknesses. Therefore, it is common for partners with a small heart energy to try to hide their gift. Watch out! If you or your partner hides "weaknesses," you will stay immature and never grow your small heart gifts into big ones. Instead, make a space for the "weaknesses" you both have, thus giving them the opportunity to become strengths.

Both strengths and weaknesses must be seen as gifts. Strengths are big gifts and weaknesses are little ones. Both are valuable! Little energies, if cherished and parented by the big strong ones, can grow into big gifts. In reality, there are no bad energies. There are only strong ones and weak ones, big ones and little ones. After all, you don't think of children as being deficient just because they are small, do you?

Creating outlets for you and your partner to express in a balanced way into the relationship is vital for both your personal and relationship health. Balance helps eliminate the overriding of smaller tokens brought to the relationship. Balance might even be considered the key ingredient to Support. Many times, over-giving is seen as Support. But in reality, Balance is the answer for supporting both strengths and weaknesses. You might say that the key to having good Balance in a relationship is acknowledging all the cards brought to the table and playing the hand well.

Becoming "half-a-person" is one pitfall to watch out for in dealing with each other's strengths and weaknesses. Usually we match up with people who are strong where we are weak, and vice versa. This is a good thing if you allow the strengths to parent the weaknesses. But, it is a bad thing if the relationship acknowledges only the strong half. If you are presently in a half-a-person relationship, you might ask yourself why you have done this. To answer this question, you will need to identify both halves — the one that is being acknowledged in the relationship and the one that isn't. Usually the half that is acknowledged is considered the strength by both partners, while the other half is considered the weakness.

Childhood Programming

If you look back into your childhood, you probably will find that your current relationship mirrors the value system of strengths and weaknesses your parents had. Your childhood programming carries over into adulthood to tell you not only what parts of you that you can offer as strengths, but how these parts should be received. That same inner childhood voice also points out every expression that was labeled as weak. To change from "half-a-person" to a whole person in a relationship, you must go back and convince your inner child that you can guarantee she or he can now have a different value system. It will be up to you to carry out that promise.

Let's say you were praised for your Willingness to try new things as a child, but never supported when you tried to be Humorous. So at some point you decided Humor was weak in you. You accepted that you were just a serious person. What we believe about ourselves is actually what we convince others to believe as well.

Tell your inner child that you have Willingness to support her or him in growing up your dwarfed energy of Humor. It is not to be ignored just because it is small. Your partner may not laugh at your beginning attempts at Humor, but remind the child that you are not trying to please your audience — you are simply acknowledging another piece of your expression. These types of steps will be necessary if your desire is to be a whole person.

Reality checks will help you
unearth the hidden enemies
while they are just
little dust balls of clutter
and can be swept up easily.

The Hidden Enemies

7

As you begin to view the purpose for relationship differently, you will begin to see more clearly the enemy patterns you have allowed to come in and violate your sacred relationship space. Such things as competition, manipulation, suppression, stagnation and denial will now stand out as rips in the fabric of your life together. Enemy patterns will be called on the carpet and labeled as enemies.

Competition

Competition sits at the top of a hidden enemy list. A small amount is of no consequence, but it can get out of hand. After all, competition is an extension of the survival instinct. It is that part of you that wants to come out on top or beat the odds. However, "topping" your partner goes directly against the purpose of your relationship to connect in a balanced way.

Competition means winning to most people. It means surviving or staying alive, even if everyone else goes down. There is no quicker way to kill "caring concern" and "willing support" than to have the competition enemy enter the scene. Competition is not an energy that can be shared. It stands alone and on top.

You know as well as I do that playful competition in a board or sports game can make it more fun. Even then, your urge to win must not override your recognition that the other person is more valuable than the game. Why even bother to play a game if you aren't sharing with someone? The desire to share is exactly why sports bars exist. Internally, sharing is more important than the ball game. You just have to make sure that the internal need to share is not blocked by the learned urge to win. Competition, when placed in proper perspective, can add a dimension of Passion that can be a stimulating addition to the sharing. But always remember, competition is not a real energy need.

Manipulation

Even though manipulation is a way of life for some people, it is a dark enemy to relationships. Manipulation comes in many forms — all with the same intent. That intent is to get other people to feel, think, or do as you want them to. Being able to convince others to turn the corner to face in your mental direction is okay if you use the frontal approach. But to sneak around behind their thinking and start tearing it down or moving it around is playing dirty.

Manipulation is definitely about playing dirty. Your partner may end up agreeing with you and even believe you are wise and wonderful, but there are no longer two real spaces being shared. You just filled up your partner's personal space with your need to be in control. It doesn't matter if you are agreeing or disagreeing; there must be two individual spaces sharing thoughts in a balanced and respectful way for a relationship to have a clear mental space.

Pushing your partner's guilt button in order to get him or her to do what you want takes you off "The Good Relationship" list. Making your partner feel guilty, along with making him or her feel sorry for you, also takes you from the good to the bad list. Naturally, you know each other's "emotional buttons." That kind of vulnerability should happen in close relationships. However, vulnerability in a relationship should be protected, not vandalized.

Unfortunately, some people in relationship haven't yet risen to the elevation of honoring their partner's feelings. They believe emotional and mental manipulation gives them power. This false sense of power seems to be worth the dishonor they are smearing all over the relationship space. For the relationship to have an emotional space, both people's feelings must be honored.

Manipulation is all about false power. It happens when one person feels the need to be in control all the time or feels out of control and thinks control must be recaptured. In the non-heartful world, control does equal power. Obviously, you aren't responsible for making your partner feel powerful, but you can define expressions of Power that leave out control and are honoring to all involved. For instance, you might refuse to argue if the same person always wins. Instead, you could define ahead of time that you would each write down your position, wait a day before responding, then start the writing process over again until there is a resolution.

Another possible solution would be to make a space for two different outcomes to every argument. Two outcomes happen when I play with my granddaughters. The older one loves to make up games and can jump from one new idea to another in a heartbeat. The younger child isn't able to think that big or that quickly. Therefore, we have defined that both children get a turn, with no criticism of their idea allowed.

Mental and/or Emotional Relationship Suppression

No one would ever admit to consciously suppressing their partner, but it happens all too often. Mental and/or emotional relationship suppression is the third hidden enemy. It is akin to suffocating someone physically. If you carried suppression out as a physical act, you might go to jail. It is such a violent thing to do to someone that no one wants to admit the capability of such an act.

This violent type of abuse is usually done through a persistent tearing down of the other person's worth. None of us is confident enough to withstand constant criticism or nagging without it doing some damage. The attackers may believe they are only telling the truth by stating how stupid or irritating the other person's habits are. But, in reality, the attackers are refusing to acknowledge their own personal need. The attackers may even know that everyone has some irritating habits, but still feel an urgency to suppress their partner's habits in order to relieve their upset feelings. If you are a nagger or criticizer and really don't want to suppress the worth of your partner, how do you stop?

Before answering that question, let's look at some of the most common complaints. Unequal amounts of Order, Cleanliness and Completion between the two relationship people oftentimes are the triggers for emotional or mental suppression. Having promised to pick up the dry cleaning several times before actually doing it, and then doing it only after you are reminded, can be an annoying pattern. Leaving the kitchen a mess after cooking can also be irritating. Seldom putting things back once you finish with them, or putting them back in the wrong place, is also bothersome. Still these and many more inequalities exist, but identifying your partner (or yourself) as being these patterns is a major relationship error.

Tearing down your partner over and over doesn't solve the problem; it only begins to suppress your partner's self-worth. Instead of thinking of that person as a stupid or irritating adult who won't cooperate, think of him or her as a child unable to do the task. Handle the situation in the same way you would with a small child. You might write up a weekly cleaning list, put the task names in a bowl, and then take turns drawing a task. This would help your partner be more aware of forms that support the energy of Cleanliness. The whole of the person is not immature; it's just his or her energy of Cleanliness that is underdeveloped.

Certainly you don't want to be in a relationship with someone who is a child most of the time. Yet everyone has undereveloped heart expressions in some areas. To support your partner in growing up immature Completion, you might write a reminder note or tie a string on your partner's finger before she or he leaves the house, just as you would do to remind a youngster.

If your partner is sloppy, you could designate one room that he or she can mess up. Or you could remind your partner to pick up things at the end of each day — just as you would support your child in developing Order. If you aren't good at keeping your money in Order and your partner is, let her or him dole out the money to you as is appropriate, and you take on another task that you do well. You are never obligated to grow a heart energy, but everyone innately wants to grow. However, no one needs to be suppressed in growth.

But don't end a "child-handling" situation with a sense of being the parent. Instead, end it by focusing on one of the person's strong points. This will help bring you back to the realization that you are two adults with just a few underdeveloped areas. Support builds self-worth — suppression tears it down.

STAGNATION

Routines can save time and eliminate stress. They are efficient and known. Yet, as with all good things, they can be carried to an extreme. It is so easy to fall into the most efficient and most effective way to clean the house, drive to work, make love, and buy the groceries. Why not if it works? The "why not" is answered by reminding yourself that Creativity, Spontaneity, Expansion and Growth are all energies that can be introduced only into changeable environments.

Efficiency and Comfort are important, but without movement, a relationship will stagnate and if not die, at least smell pretty rotten. Loyal, committed people may not even realize that they are slowly dying because doing something rash, like having an affair or going on a vacation by themselves, doesn't even enter their thinking. Don't get me wrong. I am not condoning rash behavior, but I am most definitely recommending varying the routine and throwing in a wild card every so often.

If you are not an outside-the-line type of thinker, ask a friend for some ideas. Then make sure you don't mark them all off as too "far out." Instead, let your fantasies take you beyond the idea, so when you come back to the once "far out" idea, it won't seem like such a stretch. Interject these outside-the-line plans into your life on a regular basis. Don't wait until the stagnation enemy has taken its toll by sucking the life out of your relationship.

DENIAL

The last hidden enemy I want to discuss is denial. As with all of these behind-the-scenes monsters, denial sneaks in and gradually takes over until the original Love shared becomes only a memory. Denial can strike in many different places. It can make you believe that everything is fine when, in fact, stagnation is squeezing the life out of you and the relationship. It can also hide away from your consciousness all the good that is available.

Denial can keep you from seeing how much you take responsibility in keeping the relationship afloat. While on the other hand, it can also keep you from seeing how little you contribute to the relationship. Denial is a huge enemy to the stabilizing component of balance in a relationship.

Some people are in such denial of their feelings, their intent, and even their actions, that their relationship roles all become imaginary. It is sort of like sitting on a keg of dynamite and pretending that it is candy. When your relationship gets out of balance, either it is brought back into balance, or you both must deny that there is a problem. Imbalance is too painful to ignore without the help of denial. However, denial is not the helpful friend it pretends to be.

Imagine doing any activity that requires two people — like rowing a boat or dancing — when you are physically out of balance. You will probably just feel very uncomfortable at first, but if the imbalance continues, one or both of you will get hurt. Being aware of the discomfort can abort the hurt. Stepping out of denial allows detection of the early discomforts, thus eliminating many of the hurts.

Reality checks will help you unearth the hidden enemies while they are just little dust balls of clutter and can be swept up easily. Few relationships can totally avoid every one of these hidden enemies, but many can be easily dealt with by scheduling regular checkups. Cleaning out the corners of your relationship before it gets diseased from the "filth" is no different from cleaning your house on a regular basis.

Disconcerting patterns, as well as different-sized gifts, will always be variables that must be dealt with in any relationship. How high your relationship rates on the quality graph will depend on how many tools you have available for dealing with these inconsistencies. Practice addressing the little problems and you will find that the big ones never come.

Balance requires
unselfish consideration
for what serves
the relationship best.

Balance

8

Imagine that your relationship has dealt with whatever hidden enemies were lurking around and you have traveled into smooth waters once again. The stabilizing component of Balance energy is up and running. Both of you are doing your part. The emotional waters are calm, and no one has any big complaints. Your relationship is in Balance.

It is this wonderful space of Balance (where you feel all is right with the world) that you understandably want to maintain. However, energy is always moving and life is about growth, not just comfort. You must be on the alert not to let complacency creep in unannounced. You can never really let down your guard and stop watching for signposts that indicate a curve up ahead. To keep going straight, to do what has been working over and over, without being sensitive to the need to make a turn, would be akin to living in the crater of a volcano just waiting for it to explode.

Balance is not a constant state. It is an ever-adjusting energy that requires constant vigilance. You may need to nudge one definition just a little or sometimes change several of them. Maintaining Balance in your relationship is no different than what a trapeze artist does on the high wire. The performer may need to adjust only one foot a little, or may have to move her or his whole body to avoid losing balance. Trapeze artists will do whatever it takes to stay balanced because that is what makes their act a success. The same is true in your relationship. Balance ensures success.

Mental Balance

The thinking part of one or both partners may need to adjust a little for Balance to be maintained, or it may be your actions or feelings that must make the turn in order to avoid the disaster of going straight when straight no longer works. For example, if one of you has a big fantasy expression in your thinking and the other only thinks in practical terms, then Balance may come into play by the fantasy person agreeing to tone down the fantasy state. Beware though that peace and harmony will remain the theme only until the fantasy expression begins to feel suffocated. Toning down any real expression in the relationship means you must give it an outlet elsewhere. Big expression pieces can't stay small forever. They can be less active for periods of time, but eventually they must be redefined or the enemy of stagnation will cast an evil spell over you or your partner. At a certain point in time, Balance will be able to continue only if the practical thinking person agrees to take a back seat to the expansive fantasy thinker for awhile. This, of course, means that practicality must find new places to live for that partner.

Even though the "lead relationship position" in this example may swing from practicality to fantasy and then back again, the non lead person still needs to have an expression. Remember, Balance has three spaces to work in (yours, theirs and ours). To take expression from one circle means there must be more in another. There are many possibilities of how that might look in this fantasy/practicality example — one being that the fantasy person might simply find a book that would meet his or her expression need. Or the practical person might take care of a need for practical expression by setting up two bank accounts, one for personal savings and another joint account in which both people could contribute equally.

Balance doesn't always mean sameness. You and your partner don't have to think alike to be in Balance. However, all thoughts, from both of you, must be considered. None can be thrown out unless by joint consent, but neither of you should be attached to keeping your ideas in the relationship space. Some can be designated to go into your individual spaces. Balance requires unselfish consideration for what serves the relationship best.

Emotional Balance

Emotional Balance in a relationship is just as important as thinking Balance. Again, keep in mind that Balance does not equal sameness. Also remember that in dealing with the emotional health of your relationship, all feelings have a right to exist, just as is the case with all thoughts. Even though you may try out a feeling in your relationship space first and find it doesn't fit, you still have your personal space for relocation. Don't discard a feeling just because it doesn't fit in your relationship. It is unhealthy to have your feeling nature become a flat line. Each and every feeling not only has a right to a voice, but needs to be cleared so the flow can continue. Each feeling has the responsibility of continuing the flow from an emotion to a heart energy. Use each feeling wisely.

Alive feelings are always in flux. Constant rebalancing is a must. That is not to say that when your partner is down emotionally you must be up, or that you both should be down. However, it is necessary to be aware of the emotional variables at all times. The definition of the moment must always be big enough to cover both people's feelings, but only as part of the sorting/balancing process. No feeling should be allowed to take up permanent residence in any of the three spaces. Fixation is death from any part of you — physical, emotional, mental, or spiritual.

Let's pretend that you and your partner always spend Saturday mornings in bed cuddling and talking. It has been an important sharing time for years and one of the stable definitions in the relationship. Then one day you get word that your mother is very ill. Naturally, you are upset, but at first the upset makes you want the cuddle-sharing time even more. After the shockwave passes, you begin to pull into yourself, while memories of your growing up flood your psyche. Lots of feelings are there, but they haven't shaped into words. You don't want to cuddle and share. You just aren't ready. It is time to find a new Balance point. You need to tell your partner where you are emotionally. Then the responsibility for dealing with your emotions can be assigned to your space. Sharing can be given a new form in the relationship and Balance is once again in place. If, however, you keep cuddling, but draw inward with your feelings, the relationship has an empty hole in the sharing section.

Spiritual Balance

Spiritual belief systems don't usually change at the same lightning pace that feelings do. Because of their slower pace, rebalancing can be easier, but that only holds true if the two of you are moving together on a spiritual growth path. If one of you is growing spiritually and allowing your belief system to change while the other is standing still, imbalance may be less obvious than in the other three areas — physical, emotional or mental. Since the change is more gradual, oftentimes the non-changing partner ignores the change, marking it off as just another phase, until finally reality dawns that one of you has become a stranger.

To maintain spiritual Balance when one partner's belief system changes and the other partner stays the same, the relationship space must choose to have fewer or smaller forms for expressing joint spiritual beliefs. Then, to take care of the expanded spirituality brought by the partner who has chosen a spiritual growth path, that person's individual space must now have either more or bigger forms for that expression. Conscious recognition of what is happening to each of you in your relationship is the first step to creating Balance.

When spiritual priorities get realigned in one of you but not the other, the old mental, emotional and physical forms need to be revamped. This is because a person's spiritual belief system is what determines her or his interests and priorities. Spirituality is like the eyeglasses one looks through to see the world.

Let's look at an example of how spiritual imbalance might be confronted. Both Jane and John were satisfied with the church they belonged to. Then Jane started having some dissatisfaction that led her on a quiet search for spirituality in a different form. The new form gradually caused Jane to see life from a whole new perspective. Since no one can grow in spiritual awareness without expanding awareness mentally, emotionally, and physically, all past forms became a little tight. Many of the forms Jane and John previously used to express heart energies together no longer worked, and Jane's personal space expression forms weren't working either. A mammoth rebalancing act was in order.

This rebalancing took awhile. Since John had chosen not to change his belief system, he started blaming Jane for the discomfort caused by the imbalance. He was angry because Jane had messed with the status quo. He tried to dissuade her from her new beliefs and her newly-built priorities but it didn't work. Finally, he was willing to take a hard look at what ideals could still be shared. Once these were established, then new goals and priorities were set in place that fit where the two still had a meeting of the souls.

Maintaining Balance means that both of you must be willing to let all three circles (the two individual spaces and the relationship space) change sizes. Sometimes that means that the relationship space gets smaller while one or both of your individual spaces gets bigger. Just remember, neither you nor your partner should ever be sacrificed for the relationship under the guise of maintaining Balance in the relationship. For the relationship circle to grow, both of you must first grow your individual "circles." One person growing cannot change the size of the relationship, but two can. You can't create a bigger, third relationship circle unless both of you equally contribute to it.

PHYSICAL BALANCE

Physical Balance is usually thrown askew when a new baby or a new job enters the picture. New hours, new demands, and new physical spaces all impact the relationship and require a different system of Balance.

This is the time to sort out all activities that don't have a lot of enhancement value. Keep what adds the most to the relationship even if you have to change the time spent in those particular forms or even totally change the forms.

For example, you may have to give up having coffee and crossword time together on Sunday mornings if a new baby is screaming to be fed. You could change that event to an evening time or change the form altogether by having your play time be an away-from-the-home event and having a babysitter be with the baby. Then again, working crossword puzzles together may have to become an occasional activity, and playing with the baby may become the main form of together entertainment.

In every situation that demands rebalancing, you will more than likely have to deal with some frustration or outright anger by one or both of the relationship participants. It is natural to blame your partner for upsetting the apple cart, but it is not natural or healthy to keep on blaming and being angry instead of making the necessary adjustments to restore Balance. Change is the only constant in life — and in relationships.

See your "enemy patterns"
as part of your learned behavior,
but not part of who you are.

Relationship Within Yourself

9

It is impossible to bring an undiscovered part of yourself to a relationship. Having someone else dig up all the wondrous treasures that you have buried within you probably isn't going to happen, so come with me on an inward journey to dig up the lost gems.

Most people live from other people's cast-off energies rather than discover their own. If you have squeaked by thus far in your life literally from the goodness of other people's Hearts, this is a perfect time to start bringing your part. You may have a lot of other people's rubble to sort through, but you now have a goal in mind.

Many of your inner energies have lain dormant for years, perhaps even since birth. The search for these precious parts of you may involve some painful excavation. Unless your parents were skilled at helping you to birth all of your heart energies, you probably just mimicked the expression of someone else. Or, worse yet, you mimicked others mimicking.

This brings up a very important question. How can you tell the difference between a genuine expression of a heart energy and a mimicked one? A real expression of your essence connects all the way through you from your Spirit, through your mind, your feelings, and then flows into your physical body and out into the world to create health in all aspects of your life. You may seem genuine, but upon closer inspection, you will find that you are a box of contradictions. For instance, you may seem to have an abundance of acceptance in some circumstances, but be very judgmental in others. If that is the case, then acceptance is a learned behavior that was taught to be expressed around certain areas of life. Real Acceptance, the kind that flows from your Spirit through all your other three expressive parts, is consistently present. It is who you are — meaning you are Acceptance at all times!

Let's stop for a minute to list a few of the energies of a person's Spirit that make up the real essence of who the person is. Kindness, Patience, Wisdom, Strength, Persistence, Courage, Commitment, Loyalty, Honesty, Acceptance and Support are examples. (Several are listed at the end of the book.) Plus, there are about as many different aspects to each energy as there are diversities of energies. All of these are the birthright of your Heart. It is up to you to let them teach you how they want to express through you. There is no handbook of heart energy rules that is tailored to fit everyone. Each person is a unique aspect of every single heart energy. Your energy of Kindness may be genuine in that it is a part of you all the time and runs through the totality of you; however, it may look different from your partner's Kindness. You may be kind in a gentle way while your partner may have firmness in his or her energy of Kindness. Don't try to be like your partner or insist that your partner be like you. Doing this covers the real with rubble.

You would think that clearing out the mimicked patterns of expressing in an unreal way would be easy, but that isn't always the case. Some of those learned expressions came from people with whom we share love and admiration. It seems easier to trust others that you love more than yourself because you see them as good. You know all of your flaws, so you fear you will get the bad and the good all mixed up. As a result you mimic what you see as good from the outside and hide your essence on the inside. Then, of course, there is always that little question lurking in the back of your mind that asks, "Will they still love and appreciate me if I express in different ways?"

I had one student who had so emulated her mother's expressions that she was overwhelmed when she discovered her mother's patterns didn't fit the real her. Her first attempts to be herself felt very uncomfortable, especially in her mother's presence. When she finally told her mother who she was — how her true expressions were not the same as she had always shown the family — the mother was devastated. This will often be the case with people close to you. Their first reaction will be anger that you tricked them. The anger is usually followed by fear since you are now an unknown. Next will come hurt because what they thought they loved no longer exists. The happy ending is that you will finally have the opportunity to have a real relationship.

Seldom do you hide completely from others or yourself. Therefore, confronting your mimicked patterns of expression can provide relief. The "truth" is finally being told. The best way to handle a "coming out" encounter is to treat the new part of you as if it were a young child, for in a way, it is. Introduce it to others with simplicity in little steps. Nurture it in yourself as a precious but fragile newborn. Those who truly love you will welcome what you bring, and it doesn't matter what those who don't love you think.

How to Incorporate New Energies into Your Mind

Your mind holds blueprints of how each energy you possess should look. However, all of these blueprints were not drawn to *your* Heart's specifications and therefore will not meet your needs very well. Coping is not a necessary way of life. You can assess which programmed blueprints are causing you just to get by, and then rework them until they meet your Heart's specifications. It doesn't matter how much you admired the original "architect." No one can know you as well as you know yourself — not your blood family, not your lover, not your friends.

Several years ago, I had a friend who had a large measure of Generosity around physical things. She shared her home frequently with people. If someone needed some object, she did her best to find it for them. She also was generous with her time and gave physical support to her friends' projects. I admired this energy in her greatly. In fact, I admired it so much that I tried to emulate it. To put it plainly and simply, it did not work for me to be as physically generous as she was. I didn't have her stamina, time, or money. However, when I realized it was her blueprint I was emulating, I drew up my own plans and I found I could express just as much Generosity as she did, only in a different way. The form that fit my heart energy of Generosity was emotional support instead of physical support.

Once you discover an inconsistency in what you feel is one of your genuine heart energies, name it for what it is — an imposter. Using imposters for an extended period can destroy your self image. Even though I am talking about your relationship with yourself right now, I want to stress that a major problem for couples is for one or both partners to try to become a carbon copy of the other. It won't work! Believe me, no one can impersonate another for an extended period of time. It turns sour when the imposter gets exposed.

Don't make excuses for why you failed to use a particular energy when it was needed. Instead, find out why you were afraid to use that energy or why you borrowed someone else's form, and then try again. Neither stress nor circumstances can change your basic nature if it is real. If you are mimicking heart energies, then stress and circumstances will take their toll, and your personality will suffer.

Having named an imposter expression, you can decide whether you want to turn it into a real one or not. Let's suppose that you no longer want the sporadic imitation of Patience that you acquired from your mother. You want to express Patience when you are tired and afraid just as much as when you are rested and things are running smoothly. Simply having the desire plants the seed for the real energy of Patience to grow inside you. In fact, you will begin to dislike greatly the way your mother's expression of sporadic Patience looks on you.

Of course, in its infancy, Patience won't be able to cope fully with the big tough situations, but even in its meekest approach it will be yours, not an imitation of your mother. If your deepest desire is to grow the energy of Patience, you will consciously recognize when a situation is calling for it. You will also know if the size of your Patience matches the circumstance. By holding these two important pieces of information — what is needed and what you have to offer — you will not feel lessened by the outside demand even if you cannot meet it.

The next step, after naming the imposter and choosing to grow up a real energy, is shedding all your preconceived ideas of how that energy should look. As I said earlier, your flavor of Patience, Acceptance, Support, etc., will be uniquely yours. For instance, if you hang on to a friend's belief that Kindness means you give yourself away, you might never discover that your Kindness rejects all needy, take-care-of-me kinds of requests from others so that you can be kind to yourself.

The shedding process can be scary at times because those people who haven't claimed their real energies will be threatened by anything that doesn't fit with their mimicked ones. When you are in those situations, just keep in mind that no reward can come by meeting their demands, because unreal-plus-unreal does not equal friendship.

The question may arise as to how far you can stray from the norm (usually set in place by your family) in defining your new heart energy. If, for example, you were taught that the energy of Adventure meant going on trips to new places, you might have a difficult time letting your Adventure piece define much smaller outings even though your Adventure might not even like to travel. Instead, it may prefer to read an exciting book. That is a long way from what you were taught Adventure should look like, but it is still Adventure, and you must let yours have a life of its own.

The reverse of size is true also. For example, you might need to express Nurturing in a bigger way than it was shown to you in your growing up. Your mother may have nurtured her family by baking sweet treats. However, Nurturing for you may need more forms of expression than baking. Your forms of Nurturing might be attending your child's school performances, listening to your partner sort through possibilities at a clothing store, as well as cooking for friends and family.

You have now kicked out the imposter in you that could only express Nurturing through one form. You have chosen to birth your own energy and have given it custom-tailored ways that it can express. You are now ready to be real.

Once you accept the joys of heart parenting, there will be no turning back. Perhaps you did not opt to have flesh and blood kids in this life. Not to worry. "Heart kids" are just as rewarding!

How to Introduce the New You to Your Feeling Nature

Were you trained to appreciate only physical outcomes? Have you ever stopped to consider that very little has been accomplished in this world (that has had lasting value) when feelings were not put into the effort? In other words, the good physical outcomes have a hidden secret ingredient — feelings. Take Mozart's music, for instance. It has lasted lifetimes because of the strength of his Passion that came through all of his compositions. Yes, he was gifted as a musician, but how many gifted musicians have lived that long through their music? Mozart put his feelings into his music. He possessed the secret ingredient.

Emotions in general have gotten a bad rap, and oftentimes they deserve the bad label because they are misused. People are labeled "ditzy" when they live from their emotions instead of using their feeling nature as a support. When anger becomes a weapon rather than an expression, innocent folks get victimized and the victimizer gives emotions one more bad mark. "Dreamer" is another label attached to those who are stuck in their feelings when they should be touching down to Earth.

Emotions are not meant to live alone. They are important support members of your team, but they need your Heart, mind and actions to work with them. Neither were they meant to be left out. To be without feelings on one extreme, or to be total feelings on the other, equals emptiness or misery. It is vital for your mind, body, and emotions to work with the Spirit of your being in letting you express yourself fully in life. If any one part shuts down or takes over, your expression gets blocked and a portion of you dies.

Your feeling nature not only fills each moment with substance, but it also brings sustaining value. Which memories return to you? The answer is the ones containing emotional substance. You remember people who sparked some kind of feeling in you. It doesn't matter if it is a pleasant or unpleasant feeling; the feeling association helps you remember. Advertisers know this to be true and use it constantly. Remember the singing raisin ad? If you do, it was because it activated your feelings, not because it was profound.

The sad fact is that you probably are re-creating the same emotional patterns you were brought up experiencing. If you grew up in a non-feeling household, then you probably are still limiting the colors on your emotional pallet. If, on the other hand, you grew up with intense emotions flying all about, you will keep creating people in your life who are that intense emotionally. At some point you will have to give up your hand-me-down emotional script and begin writing a new one. The new one will need to have an emotion made-to-order for every single heart energy that you have claimed.

Once you have introduced each new piece of the new you to a feeling, you then can begin tuning that feeling to harmonize with the intensity of each energy. A small energy may not have a lot of "zip" to it, while one that has been around for awhile may be more seasoned and thus have more substance. Allow yourself the space to express both quantitatively and qualitatively from your emotional body.

Only by giving up your old script can you make room for a new one. I remember how horrified I was to discover myself emotionally responding to my children in the exact same way my mother did. Not that Mother was wrong, but I was not my mother. The only other role model I had growing up was my dad, who expressed very few feelings. I was not my dad either.

All too often, grown up children believe they have only the two choices — Mom or Dad — as role models. Actually, the world is full of role models. And, while you don't want to become any one of them, you can use them as examples of expressive freedom. This helps you pick and choose what best fits you. Also, you must keep in mind while writing your new emotional script that every single heart energy needs special acknowledgment by a feeling response. Not one can be left out or it will die. Nor can you write one script and consider yourself finished. You must continually refine the old and create new emotional expressions because you are a growing, changing entity.

Feelings not only add substance to your expressions, they also let you know when a real expression is missing. Each feeling response to your outside world simply tells you how much of your Heart is expressed in that world. In other words, how much of the real you did you provide in your expression? If you expressed little, or you were out of balance because your partner expressed more or less than you, then you probably felt anger. However, if you felt in the "good range," then you more than likely expressed enough. Note that I said enough, not right. There is no one right emotional expression. There is just the one that best fits you.

The mistake you may make is in believing that circumstances outside of you create and therefore control your feeling nature. This is absolutely not true. Your feeling nature is yours. Its purpose is to support you, not victimize you. To get to the place where you experience every single circumstance as an opportunity for your feeling nature to support you, you must continually introduce the new you to your feeling nature. The old hand-me-down script must be torn up and thrown away. You may need to add more colors to your emotional pallet and gather more canvases on which to paint. Do whatever it takes.

How to Give Yourself Permission to Act Differently

Having mentally rewritten your blueprints and emotionally added more appropriate colors to the spectrum of your feeling pallet, you will want to act differently. You would think that after all the changes you have been through, acting differently would be a piece of cake. That is not always the case. Your physical body has a programmed memory just the same as your mind and feeling nature.

Did you ever learn to do something wrong, like a dance step, and then try to unlearn it? Unlearning can be much more difficult than learning from scratch. But unlearn is what you must do with many of your physical patterns that were learned by following someone else's blueprint. You must take out the old in order to put in the new.

Few people realize how robotic their lives are. They eat the way they were taught to eat. Their hygiene habits basically come from their early training. Their posture probably is a hand-me-down from one of their parents. The "old way is best" list gets added to continually. Even if at one point in time they consciously chose the fastest way to get to their job as an expression of Efficiency, they may still drive miles out of their way in order to use the same mechanic they used before they moved.

Relearning is an ongoing process, and the dark arm of habit is always lurking about to grab you back into unconsciousness. Good intentions don't seem to work. Willpower works for a short time, but who can be strong forever? How many times have you said you were going to change your eating habits and failed in the long haul?

How do you unlearn and relearn patterns of behavior? How do you retrain your physical memory to act in a conscious way to support the new you? As trite as it may sound, you will have to love yourself more powerfully than you love your old patterns.

When you read the Biblical quote, "Love your enemies," you automatically think of loving those people who are against you. Not that that isn't good advice; it is. However, I would like you to apply the quote to yourself. It is important for you to love yourself while having those physical patterns that work against letting you grow and change in the physical. You can change those "enemy patterns of action," but they cannot be changed by hating yourself for having them. For in hating the "enemy patterns," you are pushing them away from the very part of you that can bring change — the heart energy of Love.

Imagine a mistreated child, who was acting out in rather bad ways, being placed in your care. Would the child heal by your hating him or her? Of course not. You would need to see the patterns of misbehavior as separate from the identity of the child. That is the exact same way you must love yourself. See your "enemy patterns" as part of your learned behavior, but not part of who you are. If you change inwardly and your actions don't change, the inward change will atrophy and fade away. However, if you love the real inward change, then the unreal patterns will fade away.

There is more to this than tricky semantics. In one workshop, I had the participants repeat several times, "I am not my patterns." Grasping this truth will help you give up your guilt, anger, and even hate. It will help you give up all the judgment you heap on yourself and help you to replace it with Love. Then, and only then, can you give yourself permission to release your unhealthy behaviors and replace them with healthy ones.

To handle everyday problems
in your relationship,
you must acquire tools
to use in all four parts
of your being.

Handling *the* Everyday Problems

10

You now have a basic understanding that there are three spaces of a relationship — yours, theirs, and ours. You also have a clearer picture of who you are and what you have (and want) to bring to a relationship. Therefore, you are now ready to gather some tools for daily living. This is the part where you deal with the nitty-gritty of everyday problems.

There is no way you can avoid different preferences concerning physical forms, emotional upsets, and mental disagreements unless you are living with your clone — and that would be boring. In fact, it is essential that both people have unique, individual spaces in order to help each other expand and grow. However, diversity can be the cause of a relationship break-up or sometimes even a personal break-down if you try to fix problems in any one of these three areas (physical, emotional, mental) without the proper tools.

Physical Tools

A problem for some couples appears when it is necessary to speak their voice around a physical detail, such as who is going to clean up the kitchen. The non-speaker may have an inner dialogue that goes something like this: "If I ask my partner to do the dishes, she will say, 'I'm too tired; why not wait until morning?' I'll just go ahead and do them even though I feel way out of balance." The rationalizing in this scenario usually takes place when one person in the relationship hates to cause conflict. However, since inequality of voices creates imbalance in the physical part of the relationship space, this can create a bigger, more lasting problem than the momentary conflict.

Yet, on the other hand, empty participation is also a problem if you are doing something just because you are asked. It is impossible for you to bring yourself to a task if you never brought to the relationship forms that fit you. Thus, having agreeable, but empty, participation can be as big a problem as the avoiding-conflict problem. Understand that many easy-going people don't care what happens physically as long as it doesn't cause them upset or harm. On the surface, this seems like a solution rather than a problem. In reality, these "silent" people simply are not bringing their part. They are letting their partners define from their Hearts all the way to the physical while they are just being "observing participants." Even if they agree to do a non-fitting task, they still are really just observers. This non-participation does nothing to enhance the relationship, nor does it add to your personal space.

In relationship terms, being congenial around everyday physical concerns means agreeing on what and how something is to take place. It does not mean just going along with your partner's choice. Congeniality may sometimes need to follow conflict. All that matters is that an agreement be made that covers both voices equally.

If you are a tight-lipped partner when it comes to physical stuff, then it is time for you to speak up. Even if having a preference is not a big deal to you or if you know speaking up will cause a fight, still do it! Instead of hurting the relationship, you will be helping it. If, on the other hand, you are the one with "the voice," then be careful to make room for your partner's opinion.

How you speak up is tool number one. Prefacing everything with, "In my opinion," or some such owning statement will bring less push from the opposition. It also makes room for another opinion. If you are starting by stating possibilities, say so. If you think you know what you are talking about, but aren't sure, say so. In other words, be honest in the owning of your position, but have one. At the same time leave a space for the other person to have a position also.

Are you a bit confused about this concept of physical imbalance problems? It might help to tell you about a couple I know, Shirley and James. James thinks he knows how to do everything. I might interject that it's true he is pretty handy at fixing things. James has no idea that he is excluding Shirley from physical decisions. In fact, he believes that by taking over that area of their lives, he is supporting the relationship. Shirley takes care of the kids and does her daily routine, but all big physical decisions, like where they should live, what kind of car they should buy, when they will take a vacation, etc., are all taken care of by James. It has never occurred to either of them that they have a small physical relationship. After all, they eat together and have sex on a regular basis. Even though they each have individual physical spaces, their relationship entity has little physical space. Unfortunately, Shirley and James' relationship is an all-too-familiar one for lots of couples.

Every single detail of a couple's life does not need to be jointly defined. However, everything that impacts both should be talked about until an agreement is reached and carried out. Because the relationship space is created from both people's contribution around any one subject, every area that does not represent both people's heart energies is not part of the relationship space. This means that physical concerns that affect both people in the relationship must have an agreed-upon heart energy subject that has an expression form that is agreeable to both.

Just as it is necessary to have both parties participate in defining physical concerns, it is also true that the carrying out of those definitions must have a two-party participation. This does not mean that the couple needs to do everything side-by-side. What it does mean is that Shirley's job of taking care of the children needs to be seen as a contribution to the car payment just as much as James' job.

After all, the heart energy subject of both is Support. If Shirley wants to vacation near water and James wants mountains, they will work out a vacation where both people are able to receive and then gift each other. To do this, Shirley will need to talk with James until she is clear what heart energy she receives from being near water, which might be something like Peace. James will also need to get clear on why the mountains feed him — perhaps it is Strength. Then they will be able to define together a vacation that allows both people to grow from the vacation experience. Shirley and James will receive what they need and then be able to share their heart energy gift with each other.

Seeing the relationship as more important than the daily physical happenings turns everything around from the traditional view. Most people see the relationship as supporting their physical world, instead of the physical world supporting their relationship. This priority change can be a tough one, but it is most definitely a positive one. "Is this form or action going to support our relationship physically?" is a key question to answer up front. Then you will be better able to allow your partner one-half of the participation space. If you start arguing, it is probably because this priority is not in place. Remember, it will be easier to let physical preferences be heard once the physical decision is seen as a way to make the energies of your relationship stronger.

If the relationship comes first and all physical details support the good of the whole, then diversity can be an expanding, unifying aspect rather than a singular, divisive one. For example, James would want Shirley's input if he thought the physical aspects of their life together were meant to support the relationship. It would no longer be about who could do or know the most. And Shirley would no longer feel her physical part in their life together was insignificant, even though their roles might remain the same.

To summarize, the new tools you are going to apply to the physical part of your relationship are these:

1. See the physical as an energy support to the relationship.
2. Make sure both people have a voice in all decisions that impact activities of the relationship.
3. Preface your statements with something like, "In my opinion."

These three tools will help enormously in bringing physical equality to you both, as well as add an important dimension to the third circle of the relationship equation.

EMOTIONAL TOOLS

Very few people find pleasure in hurting someone's feelings. Even people who strongly emote or who confidently express their opinions don't usually do it to hurt someone. However, hurt feelings are a reality in all relationships. When that happens, there are tools to fix the hurt and strengthen the relationship.

Before looking at the healthy ways to deal with emotional upsets, let us first look at some of the common unhealthy patterns often used. The *passive-aggressive pattern* of "getting even" can naturally be a conscious choice, but more often it is an unconscious one. I recall an instance when a student of mine, we'll call him Fred, forgot to get concert reservations for his wife Susan's birthday present. She had told him on many occasions that all she wanted for her birthday was to attend that particular concert. So the dozen red roses didn't do much to cheer her up. She was hurt and angry and there seemed to be no way for healing to take place. During the next week, Fred had all his least favorite foods served to him for dinner by his hurt wife. She, on the other hand, claimed she was over her hurt within a few hours. This is clearly a case of unconscious, passive-aggressive behavior.

While emotional denial may seem on the surface like the ideal way to handle a huge upset, it is, in truth, the worst possible pattern. Someone will always be the victimizer. The *silent sufferers* are like the passive-aggressive persons in that they also choose not to own their feelings. They are different, however, in that the passive-aggressive persons act against someone while the silent sufferers turn the feelings inward on themselves.

Feelings have to go somewhere. The only place a feeling can go and be transmuted into something good is to the Heart. There, it can find the heart energy needed to heal the emotional hurt. In the case of Susan, she was emotionally hurt because she wanted her preference to have a voice in the physical. Since Fred could not offer her the heart energy of Acknowledgment, she could have claimed it from her own Heart. This would have healed the hurt feelings and made her strong in her space.

Even though the intensity of the feeling may dissipate with time, feelings don't go away without your help. Instead of dissolving, the feeling stows away in your body. One place where you find anger turned inward is gall stones. Another place people tend to store their anger is in the form of a clenched jaw or tight muscles. Fear can cause stomach upset problems, lack of energy, as well as lack of initiative. Unacknowledged sadness can lead to heart problems and depression. In other words, emotional denial is detrimental to your personal health as well as the relationship health.

You may prefer to be physically unhealthy rather than upset your husband or wife, thus choosing to dump all your feelings into your body. This kind of false sacrifice doesn't support the relationship; it only brings dis-ease. You are half of the relationship, and if your half is unhealthy, the health of the whole is compromised. Do you see how emotional denial goes beyond just one person in a relationship? The weaker and more toxic your personal space becomes, the more the relationship space will experience low energy and toxicity.

What about the *yeller-and-screamer types*? Even though the loud, vocal people feel better after the air is cleared and perhaps live longer lives, they aren't necessarily adding anything constructive to the relationship space. Let me clarify here that "loud" in and of itself is not bad. But when blaming gets thrown into the mix, then damage is inflicted on a relationship.

For those of you who yell and scream and throw blame at your partner, the partner is always seen as the enemy. For those of you who blame yourself, you are seen as the enemy. If enemies are present in a relationship space, then the safety of the space is threatened. The yeller/screamer pattern of behavior is a particularly difficult one to deal with. Having this pattern causes you to feel that if you give up blaming and being angry about what isn't there, then it is certain you will never have it. It's true, you may never have what you want from your partner, but keeping your anger and hurt attached to the other person won't make them change. It only keeps you from creating what you need somewhere else — starting with yourself.

Let's go back again to Fred and his wife. Had she expressed her hurt and anger at not getting to go to the concert on her birthday, without blaming Fred for her feelings, then she could have admitted that Fred was not strong in the heart energy of Acknowledgment. Yes, she would have liked for him to have been acknowledging in more ways than just hearing her birthday preferences, but in truth it wasn't a strong heart energy for him. However, Susan could have recognized, by the intensity of her feelings, that she needed that energy in her life. Once she discovered her need was Acknowledgment, instead of a concert, and claimed it for herself, she could have made sure that it was available in other ways. For instance, taking part in a committee at the children's school where her input would be acknowledged might have filled the bill. In doing so, her Acknowledgment would not have been attached to that particular concert on that particular day, and she no longer would have needed to deal in a passive-aggressive manner with her upset.

All feelings need to be expressed. How they are expressed is a choice. Do you realize that you have choices beyond your learned patterns of thinking, feeling and doing? You do! Where you don't have a choice is in the intensity of your feelings, and the intense feelings are the ones that will get most destructive if they aren't directed to healthy ends.

The intensity of feeling will be determined by how much of a heart gift is available. If you have an intense anger, then you have a great need for a particular heart energy. When someone dies who was important to you, you may feel a lot of sadness. That probably means there was Love available there that you haven't fully claimed in your Heart. More than likely, you haven't claimed it because you are still attached to the physical forms that it comes through. By noting the upside of emotional intensity, you will be able to gauge the size of the heart energy available in any situation. Since the intensity of feelings tells you how much heart energy you are or are not expressing, both voices bring an equally important message.

Whether you choose to talk, yell, write, sing, or whisper your feelings, it is up to you and your partner to decide. Just keep in mind that there must be some form of expression to avoid a build-up of toxic clutter. Silent enemies left behind damage your health and the health of the relationship.

After the feelings are all out on the table, the owner must sweep away the debris to uncover the truth about the real need. The real need will always be an energy of the Heart. I mentioned the energy of Acknowledgment as being one of Susan's needs. I am sure Susan's need list is longer than one heart energy, but at that time, her principle need was Acknowledgment. Energy needs won't go away until they are addressed, so you can't just ignore them. You can, however, choose forms for their expression. Remember, you own them; they don't own you.

One of the best awarenesses to have around emotions is to know that no one can meet all your needs. You are the one who is responsible for transmuting all your feelings into heart energies. It is nice when your partner participates with you in sharing a heart energy through an agreed-upon physical form, but it is not a "have to." Once you both agree to share a heart energy in a specific way, make sure that agreement is honored. When it is not honored, a discussion needs to take place about why it wasn't. The lack of completion around your agreement will mean a need didn't get met. Unmet needs shrink spaces!

MENTAL TOOLS

Few couples hold the same meanings around words. The word "commitment" for one partner may mean lots of time spent together, while for the other, it might mean complete honesty about what is going on inside of them. "Completion" for one may mean, "I said I'll do it and I will eventually, so don't bug me," while the "bugging" one may believe completion should happen without any gaps of time in between the agreeing to do something and the doing.

It is extremely important to develop a stored mental dictionary containing the different word definitions of your partner. You can't just jabber on in "your language" and expect to be understood without covering the thinking of the other person.

It helps to have phrases in your mental library to use to support communication such as, "What did you hear me say?" or "What will help you?" Another handy tool that will help you avoid the deadly sin of assumption is to mentally catalogue past conversations on a particular subject. Remember what your partner's response was in an interaction. What meanings did the words carry?

Wrongfully assuming you covered all the bases with your words and assuming the other person's meaning and yours are the same will cause unnecessary breakdowns in the relationship space. Staying on the same communication road when it is the wrong one will take you nowhere. Imagining that your partner speaks another language will help you pay close attention to the nuances and multiple meanings.

Much communication confusion can be avoided by bringing more clarity to your words, but, most importantly, you will need to make sure the words are in resonance with your intent. Intent points directly back to the personality of a person's particular heart energy. So when you ask for a rerun on how your words were received, be sure the meaning of the key words used is perceived correctly, but also make sure your intended energy was covered.

For example, you might ask your partner to help with dinner. But you don't state now or later, you don't state what form you want the help to take, and you don't say why you want help. Step one will be filling in all the blanks with detailed words that both people understand. Then, the intent step needs to be taken. Here is where you discover what heart energy (or intent) is motivating the meal. Is it Health, Creativity, Partnership, or Communication? Communicating the intent will make a huge difference in the success of the meal.

Often the problem lies in your inability to know your own real intent. If you tell yourself you are asking for help in the kitchen because you are running out of time, when really you are frustrated because you feel there has been no energy of Support lately, the relationship will have no mental space. Your real intent is to create Support, but your "denial intent" is to get the food on the table quicker. Since you aren't giving correct information through your words, you have created a no-win situation. Your words will not allow your partner to be in a mental space with you because you are not offering the real mental subject.

So let's pretend that your partner assumes you really mean that you need a rush job on dinner and comes to offer help. The helping partner may even ask what needs to be done. This exchange of words, without the intended heart energy, can't create an exchange of real energy between you and your partner's mental energy centers. Even though you are being given exactly what you need in physical form, you can't receive it energetically because you have not mentally defined a space for it. Instead, you just put an unreal clutter of words in the relationship space. Clarity of words helps communication only when the words are created from the truth of your Heart's intent.

Of all the possible tools you might use in handling everyday mental mix-ups, I would say the first and best is to bring a double dose of honesty to your intent, i.e., what heart energy is behind your words? Next, you need to start a dictionary in your head about how the mental receptors work in your partner's mind. Then, be sure to check what was heard by your listener, even if you believe you did an excellent job of communicating.

Spiritual Tools

The most supportive tool available for the spiritual part of you is having an openness to change. The second most needed tool is being willing to let go of attachments. These two tools can turn difficult problems into beautiful growth experiences. However, being willing to turn loose of objects is hard enough; turning loose of a piece of your relationship can sometimes be excruciating. It may feel as if you are losing a part of yourself, even though, in reality, you will only be giving up a pattern or form that no longer fits. And, as an added benefit, you will get a brand new or refurbished replacement.

The tools of change and letting-go get handicapped in their implementation when you begin to act as if any one part of your life, rather than your Heart, is the center. Not that your relationship, job, kids, health, pet, etc., aren't important. They are! But the only center-point you can have in any relationship or activity (and be spiritual) is a heart energy. These heart energies can then radiate out into all areas of your life to bring richness, change and growth.

Working outward from the center-point of the Heart means that you won't say or do anything unless the words or actions carry a heart energy. It means that all the people and activities of your life are only vehicles for your Heart's expression.

Thus, your primary relationship should be solely for the purpose of uniting two Hearts into one. It is this resonating of heart energies that causes them to grow. It is this heart growth that necessitates change. And it is change that brings continual richness and fullness to your life.

In order to use your spiritual tools of detachment and change in your relationship, you will need to use them in your personal space also. It seems reasonable that there would be little difference in applying the same tools both places. However, you may find that trying to preserve your familiar personal space feels safer than detaching from old habits and emotional "warm-fuzzies" that have been your constant companions for years. Just the thought of letting go of your private, personal habits can seem daunting! After all, your relationship attachments have had a much shorter life span than your personal ones.

Unless the Heart is the center-point in your personal space, you will not have any way of reaching into the relationship space. This means that your personal process of growth must be ongoing. You can, at the same time, have a relationship growth process — in fact you should — but clearing out the old attachments to make room for the new ones in your personal space must be a priority. And that will happen only if the Heart is the center-point of your life.

It might be worthwhile to talk a little about how you can have these two parallel universes, so to speak, running at the same time. The path of personal growth begins when you get in touch with your inner desire to be more and share more. When you extend that desire to include wanting to be more and share more of yourself with another, you have created a second path of growth. Unfortunately, that desire oftentimes gets translated into doing more and giving more rather than being more and sharing more. But you now have the insight to recognize real "being" as heart energies, and real sharing as the resonating of those heart energies. Therefore, it can only mean one thing: your Heart is the current, your space is the generator, and your relationship is the receptor.

In most scenarios, the receptor is usually the ending. This is not the case in relationship. Since a relationship is an entity unto itself, it has the power to take what it receives from both people and bind the two energies together into a united, larger, more powerful vibratory energy. It is vital that both of your personal spaces and the relationship space all be functioning at the same time for the relationship to be an active receptor that gives back in large measure to the two personal spaces.

Ellen and Frank share the energy of Mission in their relationship by working together to help grow the planet's consciousness around environmental issues. The power of their separate intents has combined into a great force. This force around their relationship's energy of Mission then comes back to each of them individually. As a result, both Ellen and Frank are discovering their personal jobs to be more fulfilling because they now see how these too can carry the energy of Mission.

Once you are able to see how your space and the relationship space feed each other, it will be much easier to attend to both, without feeling one takes away from the other. Even though the issues or problems facing one space don't seem to relate to the other, they always do. In fact, you may need to give yourself or your partner some space to figure out how a particular circumstance relates to all three spaces (yours, theirs, and ours) before you can proceed. To handle everyday problems in your relationship, you must acquire tools to use in all four parts of your being — physical, emotional, mental and spiritual. Having tools at your disposal to deal with a problem at its beginning point saves much time, effort and heartache. All too often, couples wait until a problem is demanding attention before they acknowledge it. Not only does this approach create stress on the relationship, but it allows the little problems to go unnoticed. Pretty soon, several problems that could have been dealt with easily, if caught in the beginning, flare into big "fires." Before you know it, your life is consumed with putting out fires. To avoid having a relationship that is continually in "fire-extinguishing mode," keep these tools handy and use them daily.

Relationship size is determined by how well you cover each other's particular brand of like energies, not by how many you can "match."

Heart Energy Possibilities

11

While there are a multitude of heart energies that you and your partner could share, I'd like to point out eight that are wonderful supports in the relationship arena. They are Acceptance, Love, Nurturing, Support, Honesty, Trust, Generosity, Community and Commitment.

ACCEPTANCE

The heart energy most needed and most often missing in relationships is Acceptance. It is extremely difficult to give up wanting friends and partners to fit neatly into your world of thoughts, feelings and activities in order for you to accept them. The coin flips to the other side when you try to fit into their space in order to get Acceptance. Even though this flip-flopping, pseudo-acceptance doesn't resonate between two Hearts, it is still often confused for the real thing. Obviously, mimicking each other isn't going to build a real and honest relationship.

I'm sure that the lack of Acceptance has caused you a few wounds in your lifetime. If you escaped unscathed, consider yourself lucky. However, for those who didn't get their needed Acceptance fill, hiding under the seeming safety of pseudo-acceptance isn't going to solve the problem. Having to be like someone else to be accepted pretty much cancels out the real you. Similarly, the other side of pseudo-acceptance happens when you are expecting and even demanding that others be like you in order to receive them into the fake arms of your Heart. This cancels out any realness in them.

Canceling each other is just the opposite of what you need to be doing in order to create a relationship. In order to bring genuine Acceptance into your relationship, you will have to get in touch with how much fear you have of being hurt by someone not liking you. Multiply that fear by 100 and you will come close to how much you fear non-acceptance coming from your partner. That much fear lurking in your unconscious mind will train you to be a master of pretend realness. After all, don't you feel safer when you are hiding the real you? It doesn't hurt nearly as much if your partner, whose love you want, disapproves of a pretend you.

I remember well one of my first efforts of offering my real self to a group and stepping away from the expected protocol of sameness. It was in a support group setting where Honesty should have been the intent. However, everyone was just pretending to be deep and sincere. No one had pulled off the illusionary veil of alikeness that made everyone comfortable. One night, I slipped out from under the veil and shared an extreme intuitive experience.

The response to my real revelation was startling. One person, who had become a close "friend" while we were mimicking each other, never spoke to me again outside of the group. A couple of others pulled further into their shells. The good side to this story is that two of the twelve people became real friends. The value of those two real friendships far outweighed the loss of the other ten pseudo-relationships.

It would seem on the surface that having a so-called "intimate" relationship would eliminate the pseudo-acceptance approach. Since no one can pretend 24 hours a day, even pretend people will show their partners real parts some of the time. However, master pretenders have learned how to make the unreal seem real and the real seem unreal.

Since pretend people (the ones without true Acceptance) put the same kind of restrictions on others as they put on themselves, coming out to them is usually not a satisfying experience. However, to have a real relationship, you must courageously step forward and be you if you want Acceptance to grow in your relationship. Even if your partner is shocked at first, he or she will more than likely come around sooner or later.

Acceptance may be one of the hardest heart energies to bring forth, but it is also one of the most satisfying once it is obtained. If you fear judgment, you will probably have many parts of your hidden self that will need to be uncovered. Do not despair! You can reach deep down inside yourself and touch self-acceptance. You can do that by recalling those times you felt what you brought was worthwhile. Just that small beginning will be enough to help you know that judgment is empty and powerless to hurt you. Be willing to stand in the face of judgment with your Acceptance shield and you can win the battle.

Love

A second highly desirable spiritual quality to have in relationships is Love. You might be a bit surprised to see Love listed second when most people put it on the top of their must-have list. The reason Love gets second billing is because you can't really love the parts of a person that are hidden under the shadow of pseudo-acceptance. Those parts may not irritate you, but they don't grow the heart energy of Love in your relationship either.

If Love rates so high on the "I want" charts, then why is it so hard to come by? In addition to the not-too-common commodity of Acceptance being needed as a precursor, there is the handicap known as emotional attachments. When there are attachments, Love is paralyzed. There can be no change. In fact, emotional attachments falsely lead you to believe that your partner doesn't love you if he or she changes or asks you to change.

Love is a growing, changing energy. To love a child, for example, you must allow her or him to unfold into an adult. To attempt to keep a child under your protective wing simply says that you are emotionally attached to what that child brings to you, but you don't really love the unfolding person underneath. Unfolding people are not always easy to love. You really do have to give up wanting people to be a certain way in order to love them.

Since Acceptance and Love work closely together, we may need to spell out their differences. Let's say that your friend has started to speak up about his or her own preferences. While you have no problem accepting this new part of your friend, it is difficult to take a back seat to his or her choice to play tennis three times a week instead of going to the gym with you, as was the practice in the past. If you are emotionally attached to sharing that activity with your friend, you may have trouble loving the new person. In fact, you may hate that your friend has become so independent, while at the same time know (accept) that this is a good thing for him or her. Hopefully, Acceptance will win the battle, but if the emotional attachment stays strong, you have some inner work to do.

Since this attachment is able to block out loving your friend's new independence, how do you get rid of it? You will need to separate her or his new independent spirit from the activity. You can still feel the loss of your friend's company at the gym, while at the same time love his or her new zest and courage in making new and different choices.

NURTURING

Nurturing is another heart energy that can be supportive in a relationship. While it is not as crucial as Acceptance and Love, it certainly can add a glow to any partnership. What makes Nurturing so difficult is its diversity. Nurturing to one person may mean jogging together or working out together in the gym, while to another it may mean having his or her feet massaged or taking a bath together. Once again, it is vital that you know what forms the energy is best packaged in for the other person. Then you can decide if Nurturing is a heart energy you can participate with in your relationship, or if it must be kept solely in your separate space.

The preferential packages may differ, but the energy of Nurturing always serves the same purpose. Its intent is always to bring nourishment to the soul through pleasurable physical activities. In relationship, this type of soul nourishment strengthens whatever heart energy is joining you and your partner at a particular time.

It is important that the pleasurable activity support the heart connection it is nourishing. For instance, listening to quiet music could be an activity choice when both people are experiencing Peace or Relaxation. On the other hand, hard rock music wouldn't fit.

Self-nurturing outside your relationship simply means that a connection to your own Heart can be strengthened through a pleasurable activity. Nurturing is important, but as you can clearly see, it doesn't have to come in a relationship package.

Nurturing in your relationship may or may not be the same for either of you when alone. For example, you may nurture each other by sharing the heart energy of Play through the activity of being in a pool of water, while that same activity may not be Nurturing for either one of you individually. On the other hand, one of you may be fed (nurtured) by the heart energy of Sacredness through the activity of meditation, while the other may be nurtured around the Sacredness that comes through the activity of gardening. Meditation and gardening are compatible enough to fit together as a relationship expression of Sacredness.

Given that Nurturing is simply about feeding your soul by expressing a heart energy through a pleasurable activity, nurturing your partner may mean that you participate in an activity that isn't at the top of your preference list. However, you can still receive the benefit of sharing a heart connection. When there are different preferences around the nurturing activities, you may need to take turns to stay in balance. But remember, Nurturing won't happen without the heart connection firmly in place.

SUPPORT

Another nice addition to a relationship is the heart energy of Support. Just as with Nurturing, Support needs to make its way into physical form, but physical support without any heart Support behind it is not very valuable. Likewise, heart Support that doesn't also support you physically is pretty useless.

Believe it or not, Support doesn't have to match a chosen activity, as Nurturing does. When your partner asks for Support concerning a particular area, the field is more open than you might think. For example, if your partner needs Support around moving his or her office from one room to another, there are several options that fall under the broad heading of office moving. Your partner may need help with the heavy stuff, but your back is bad, so that option is out. Instead, you may offer to move the books one small stack at a time. Another option would be to offer your Support by calling in friends to help.

When children are involved, Support is often asked in a specific form. Say you are asked to pick up the kids after school because your partner, who usually does it, is going to the dentist. But you have an important meeting with a client. Don't let a specific form stop you. Instead of saying no, explore other energy of Support by asking a neighbor to pick them up or by suggesting they spend the night with a friend.

The energy of Support is threatened by routine. After a grand opening, it oftentimes gets dropped. It is all too easy to get into a physical routine and forget to fuel those daily tasks with the energy of Support. Another threat to Support is obligation. Doing something because you feel you should leaves little room for your Heart to express.

Remember, relationships thrive when the focus is the energy of the Heart. The more heart energy you can share, the stronger your relationship will become. This works until the pressures of life crowd in to overtake your original intent to Support each other with good energies. So post reminder notes in prominent places to remind you that real Support must have energetic backing.

Honesty

While Honesty is a must for some, and a preference for most, it is not an energy of necessity for everyone. Some people just plain don't want to know everything that is going on. I watched a friend of mine look the other way while her husband was having an affair. She didn't want Honesty. It would have required a response she wasn't prepared to make.

If Honesty is a heart energy that you value highly, then I suggest you define it clearly with your partner. For, as with all energies, Honesty takes different shapes with different people. For some people factual Honesty is what it's all about. For others, emotional Honesty takes top rating, while some people think doing the right thing tells the tale when it comes to being an Honest person.

I had a client who felt that being Honest was about doing what he felt was right. His wife, on the other hand, believed that agreed-upon details constituted Honesty. They would talk and agree. Then he would go do what he felt was the right thing to do. Most of the time, his doing wasn't in keeping with their agreed-upon details. She would get furious and feel lied to. He would try to explain that the circumstances demanded something different from what they had known when they talked.

They both were honest — just in different ways. So they couldn't have Honesty as part of their relationship even though they both wished it could be. Still, they both were honest people. For the man in this story to maintain his personal Honesty, he couldn't go along with his wife's definition of Honesty. For her to maintain her Honesty and not be angry with him all the time, she had to stop planning with him how things were going to be done. She either had to turn it over to him or take charge herself.

It's quite common for people to have differing views of Honesty. As with another couple I worked with, the wife felt that emotional Honesty was the primary ingredient in being totally honest. For her, Honesty was the sharing of all intimate feelings with each other. Her husband, on the other hand, believed like the man in the other example. As long as he didn't do anything wrong, he was Honest. He argued that having feelings for another woman was not dishonest, as long as he didn't have sex with her. Not surprisingly, his wife had a difficult time accepting his form of Honesty. Therefore, Honesty could never become part of the defined relationship space.

As I am sure you are beginning to see, Honesty isn't as easy to cover in a relationship definition as some of the other heart energies. Covering Honesty together isn't the same as going down a list of preferred forms until you both agree on one. Honesty (or dishonesty) is a basic part of everyone's character. It is not an activity you can share or even a task you can do for someone. However, you must make sure there is a definition that fits the character traits of Honesty for both of you before you claim it to be part of your relationship.

Trust

Trust is an energy that is hard to identify. You cannot trust a person's actions, thoughts, or feelings. You can only trust what is real and constant — the Heart. That means you have to be able to recognize the Heart. Since each and every heart energy comes in a multitude of shapes and sizes, it takes a person with deep perception to see into another person's soul. And that is exactly what Trust is all about — seeing into another person's soul.

To trust a person does not require passive acceptance of everything your partner says and does. In fact, to trust the real means you must distrust the unreal. So the definition around Trust in your relationship may include calling each other on being unreal. For example, you may ask your partner not to use an endearing name when expressing anger with you, such as "Honey, will you please move so I can empty the dishwasher?" when what's really meant is, "Will you get out of my way so one of us can get something done?"

As less and less unreal moments are allowed to exist in your relationship, more and more Trust can enter. No one likes to be on guard continually, especially when at home. So my suggestion would be to choose one or two areas of expression in which you want to grow Trust in the relationship, and monitor those areas until they become trustworthy. You may choose to start Trust around a non-threatening energy such as Play or Spontaneity. Then move to more complex ones such as Loyalty or Honor. To take on all parts at once is too much.

Generosity

What a beautiful gift the heart energy of Generosity brings to the world. However, it doesn't always seem beautiful to a non-generous partner. When the Generosity extends outside of the relationship — and it will if it is real — the non-generous partner may get jealous and resentful that it is spilling outside of the relationship boundaries.

Generosity is more than just giving things away. It is an energy that generates flow. A generous person understands that hoarding or trying to receive more than you give, is nothing more than a wastefulness of energy. When energy is not allowed to flow through a balanced giving and receiving cycle, it gets stale and dark. Even Love can become selfish if it is not allowed to flow freely.

If you both have the energy of Generosity to bring to the relationship, you can then jointly decide what to share and with whom to share it. However, if only one of you has Generosity as part of your heart package, then it needs to be defined individually in such a way as to not impact the relationship. For instance, money would not be lent to a friend out of joint funds.

Generous people need to be very careful to make sure their giving comes back in a balanced way, or they can stop their flow by over-giving. For example, you might want to buy all the uniforms for your child's ball team. This is fine as long as you can afford it and there is a return of some kind — such as Appreciation. If you do it just because you think they need them, then there is no return, and your expression of Generosity is out of balance.

These principles around balanced flow for one person also apply to the relationship. If you and your partner invite friends over for supper repeatedly and they do not return the invitation, you need to look to see if there is some other kind of return. Naturally, if you are generous, then giving always feels good. But just feeling good doesn't always mean it is a balanced act. Perhaps your friends do not have the resources to invite you to their house, but they offer you lots of Humor and Play. This could make for a balanced flow. Just make certain that there is a return, and they aren't taking advantage of your Generosity.

Community

A relationship should be a community. After all, the word community means a group of people linked by a common interest. In fact, being in a relationship helps prepare you for the more expanded version of Community. Once the energy of Community has filled your relationship space, it will naturally want to take you beyond one other person. This is a time when the two of you might join with a larger group that has interests that fit with your relationship interests.

As I said, a relationship should be a community, but all relationships are not. Again, as with any heart energy, Community must be brought by both people for the relationship to be a container for that energy. The absence of Community in your relationship tends to create a vacuum. The relationship can't reach out and cover others. It simply stays as two people doing things together. You might be saying, "What is wrong with that?" Well, what is wrong is that your relationship doesn't get to profit from having new energies infused into it from other people. All the expansion must then come solely from the two of you.

Since a relationship is a living entity, it needs growth just like any living entity. And yes, the relationship can grow if both partners are growing, but the more facets to any one heart energy you have available, the faster you can grow. You can't keep your relationship under lock and key, any more than you can a child, and expect it to be healthy. Therefore, Community is a very important energy to bring to your relationship.

COMMITMENT

Commitment in a relationship means that you both will uphold the heart energies you have agreed to share together. It means that you will support what is real and not the unreal. You are not to be committed to the other person. Instead, your Commitment is to the relationship. To say you are committed to a person means you agree to resonate with the person's unreal patterns as well as the heart-filled ones. Even committing to support only the individual heart energies of your partner (not the unreal patterns) is not the same as bringing Commitment to the relationship. Bringing Commitment to your relationship guarantees that it will stay pure.

You cannot be committed to your relationship and support your partner in his or her individual space unless you are first committed to yourself. Once you surround your life with Commitment, you will welcome any and all interactions with your partner as indicators of how real or unreal you are being. If you are sharing from a real space, you will be able to tell if your partner is right there with you or not. If there is no connect, it is time to check who went astray.

The trick to a correct reality check is listening inside instead of taking your reading from what is taking place verbally or physically. Once you discover any falseness within yourself, you can discard it and call on Commitment to help you hold steadfast to what is real and true for you. If the sense of falseness persists, then it is time to do a reality check on the relationship. Bring Commitment to the truth and purity of what is real in the relationship, and it will stay vital and alive. Keeping your relationship real requires constant Commitment. Believe it or not, two very "not-pure" people can still be committed to bringing only their best pieces to the relationship.

The shape your relationship can take is as varied as snowflakes. The list of possible heart energies you can bring to a relationship is limited only by the energies you share and hold as important. The ones talked about in this chapter (plus Communication and Balance that have already been discussed) are energies that many couples put at the top of their "want list." Your list doesn't have to match anyone else's, but you do need to have one. After you and your partner make out your "must-have list," you then will be able to choose which heart energies match and which ones complement each other. Relationship size is determined by how well you cover each other's particular brand of like energies, not by how many you can "match." A good relationship doesn't mean that it has a large number of energies in it. In fact, I have found that for most people, if you choose more than three relationship energies, you lose focus on your agreed-upon definitions.

The shade of your relationship
depends upon
how the patterns are handled.

Eliminating the Dark Side of Relationship

12

When Bad Patterns Show Themselves

It stands to reason that seemingly good relationships can turn bad or there wouldn't be so many break-ups and divorces. As with all relationships, you had to go through the courting stage where both of you were trying to entice the other by showing your very best patterns. Next, came the honeymoon period where each of you decided to be together and share these "excellent" patterns. Unfortunately, you couldn't keep all of your "bad" patterns hidden forever without becoming split personalities or acting out the "good" and "bad" parts of yourself with different people. Of course, master pretenders who make the unreal seem real (and vice versa) keep up the front longer. However, neither of these profiles fits with our concept of a healthy, growing relationship. Let's assume you are not a split personality, but a whole person. This means that, little by little, all your patterns will be known to your partner. As the two of you show more and more of your patterns to each other, the relationship can either become brighter or darker. The shade all depends on how the patterns are handled. It is rare for both people to like all of the patterns presented by the other. In fact, it is rare for anyone to like all of their own patterns. Thus, for your relationship to move on to the next stage, you must learn how to make lemonade out of lemons, symbolically speaking.

Often it takes someone acting from a distasteful pattern to bring out your best. I am reminded of a couple who were the proverbial odd couple. One was overly neat and clean while the other considered finding a needed piece of paper from the pile on the desk the ultimate in organization. Obviously, this was the germinating ground for judgment and frustration. However, the differences were handled in such a way as to bring light to the relationship rather than darkness. The disorganized, messy partner praised the orderly, clean one and offered a willingness to grow those energies. The neat, clean person started with small steps to meet their partner's request to grow, and refused to walk down the dark path of judgment about her partner's disorganization.

This setup sounds ideal, except for the danger of creating a parent-child relationship rather than an adult-to-adult one. So we go back to the key of all good relationships — Balance. The disorganized, messy partner had strong energies of Adventure and Play that the perfectionist partner admired. Steps were also put in place to gently lead the neat, clean perfectionist into a more relaxed and expanded space. Thus, the parent-child stigma turned into two adults helping each other to become more. They turned lemons into lemonade.

THE POSSESSION TRAP

Another darkening cloud comes when you try to turn your partner into a possession. I am not referring to the pattern of domination. This is about the adoration type of possession. Even though any kind of possession — adoration or domination — is dark, it is the adoration kind that most people would die to have. Beware! Possessive adoration is usually under-girded with either jealousy or inadequacy, both of which create dark energy in a relationship.

Usually idolized people enjoy and may even appreciate being put on a pedestal, but they also feel an obligation to those who are bowing down before them. The combination of need from the adorer and obligation from the adored creates a situation of ownership and owe-ership. The adorers must have the adored or there is nothing of worth left in their world. The adored feels obligated to be there for the other and thus creates a self-imposed prison.

This type of relationship effectively shuts out the world. The partners do everything together even if it doesn't really work for either of them. They feel they must pretend to enjoy times together when they really don't. After all, both people have to keep up their roles if this dark definition is to stay in place. Misplaced adoration creates a dark space of need and obligation. Neither the space of need nor the space of obligation contains any heart energies, and therefore cannot create a place of light in the relationship.

When one partner idolizes the other, no balance can be achieved. This doesn't mean that both people shouldn't bring respect and devotion to the other — they should. But one of the two can't be put on a pedestal while the other bows down. Balance doesn't happen unless both people are on equal footing.

The "I-hate-you" Prison

The seeming opposite of the adoration trap is the "I-hate-you" prison. It, too, creates a dark space in your relationship. The "I hate you's" usually occur after several years of putting up with things that bothered you about the other person. While it might seem at the time that not dealing with the little bothers was the best course, in the long run it always proves otherwise. Little bothers can turn into huge, angry prison wardens that allow very little freedom.

This kind of built-up negativity will eventually crowd out the light spaces and create big, dark spaces in your relationship. As bad as this sounds, it is not necessarily the end of the road. Even though it usually takes a relationship counselor to create a safe enough space for all the built up "sludge" to get cleared out, there is still hope. Hope only ends when the two of you pass through the "I-hate-you" stage and proceed into the "I-could-care-less" stage.

Yelling, screaming, and complaining may happen if you don't find other ways to get the backed-up residue out. That isn't always a bad thing if there is no violence and the intent is to get to a healthier place. However, guidelines as to how health is to be accomplished must be set in place for the yelling and screaming to be profitable. Guidelines are not rules for the other person to keep, but instead they are road markers put in place to guide you both in moving from old stuck darkness to new freeing light.

If your frustration has grown to a loud crescendo, but your partner is just mildly frustrated, then your partner will believe the relationship is in trouble because of your anger. This finger pointing must stop. This could be one of the first road markers towards the light. Once both of you accept that you have equally contributed to putting the relationship at the "I-hate-you" stage, then negatives can be voiced without finger pointing.

The second road marker out of the dark side is acknowledging what you can change and what you can't change at a particular point in time. Change is in order if the relationship is to survive, but both of you must agree to change. It can't be dumped on one. The point to remember at this time of change is what you agreed to at the first road marker, which is that both of you are responsible for the health of the relationship. That means both you and your partner must define what and how much you will change and then decide together what that will look like in the relationship space.

The third road marker is finding something you can do together that will give you new tools for living life differently. Beyond counseling, there are books, classes, workshops and sharing groups that can provide new tools. Your education does not end when you finish school. Actually, a good education should be about opening you up to learn for the rest of your life. Living life with another person should be one of those ongoing learning experiences.

The fourth and final road marker requires redefining what heart energies your relationship can have (not should have) right now and adjusting your needs accordingly. This may mean giving up some empty forms or adding some new forms, but having a definition keeps clarity alive and well.

Do I Still Love You?

Love will take many shapes during the life of a relationship. There will be okay shapes, special shapes, not-so-wonderful shapes, and sometimes even heavy shapes. If you are someone who wants love always to be a fresh bouquet of flowers, you may have a difficult time weathering the not-so-flowery shapes.

Allowing the energy of Love to reshape as time goes by doesn't mean giving up all your daydreams of what you hope to have in your relationship. It simply means you must stay alert to which daydreams fit you and which ones don't. You may find yourself holding onto daydreams that no longer express who you have become. When that happens, even if the daydreams become a reality, they won't bring happiness.

Daydreams that do fit *who* your relationship has become can then be goals that encourage you to keep the relationship changing and new. Moving toward new goals keeps you from feeling stuck in a not-so-flowery shape of Love. For instance, if one of you goes through a period of time in which you must spend extra hours at work, your daily sharing aspect of Love may soon shape into a little lump. If sharing still fits, but just isn't feasible at this time, you might set a goal to take a trip together after the work project is complete in order to re-empower the sharing-Love shape.

Let's say your daydream contains laughing and being silly together. That shape may become invisible after a loved one dies. You might not want to set a goal to have that particular part of your Love picture restored. Instead, a better fit during your grieving period might be to let your movie rentals have a higher percentage of comedy.

The important thing to keep in mind is that Love changes as you and your partner change. And the change of circumstances makes it necessary to re-evaluate your expressions of Love. Real Love never goes away. However, it does need support to maintain its space in your busy lives. The best support you can bring to your Love space is to periodically re-evaluate your daydreams in light of your present circumstances, as well as take stock of who each of you has become. You can then set appropriate goals to keep the relationship moving forward and in the right direction.

Am I Still Attractive?

This dark phase usually happens at the time in your life when age begins to show somewhere in your body. Either your stamina wanes, your skin begins to wrinkle, or your muscles lose their tone. No matter how many vitamins, creams or gyms you use, your attractiveness seems to be on an uncharted trip south.

As natural as this occurrence is in everyone's life, it still can be extremely traumatic. There is little anyone can do to change this direction, but still, many try. Some people try to find reassurance that they are still attractive by flirting or even having an affair. Others push harder to accomplish more at work so they feel that they are attractive in some way, even if it isn't still happening in the looks department.

As absurd as some of the antics of an aging person may be, few antics are as bad as projecting your unattractiveness onto your partner. This behavior can play out when you see only your partner's physical flaws instead of his or her inner beauty. At this stage, all the internal things that attracted you to this person get lost under the cloud of what is no longer externally there.

However, if this stage of life is used appropriately, your appreciation for your partner can deepen. The original physicality of your relationship may take a back seat to the deeper qualities that have evolved through the years. Discovering the inner beauty in yourself, your partner, and in the third entity of relationship will be a true milestone in your growing-up process. While maturity is much more than getting older, getting older can be a great impetus in claiming maturity.

Whoops! One of Us Didn't Grow!

The darkest dark side of any relationship is discovering that you and your partner are no longer equal sizes. Rarely are two people equal in all areas, even in the beginning. Usually one is smarter than the other. One may be more physically competent than the other. Emotional and spiritual development also must be factored into this equation. In the beginning, there is usually a balance between one or two of these four aspects (physical, emotional, mental and spiritual). And hopefully as time goes on, each of you will develop new parts so that the balance may be increased to three or even all four of these aspects. However, this growth is not always the direction both people take.

So what happens when one of you stays the same and the other one grows? The answer is that a scary, big, dark space fills in where the undeveloped half of your relationship exists. The non-grower may have filled the part of relationship space in the beginning, but the grower moved on while the non-grower went backwards. People either grow or shrink. No person can maintain a flat line. Thus, a non-grower creates a dark space when partnered with a grower. The only exception is when a continuous downsizing of the relationship space has happened to achieve balanced points along the way. Believe me, it can be a big shock to wake up one day and realize you are married to a "dwarf."

Let's say that what I just described is your scenario. Can this marriage be saved? Yes, but only if both of you take certain steps in the right direction. The wrong direction, but the most commonly taken road, is the one marked "Instant Growth." In this scenario, you try to force instant growth on your partner. Remember that even if your partner starts growing after receiving a wake-up call, he or she may not get caught up with where you are on your growth path for quite a while.

A second commonly chosen road is the one marked "Shrink Wrapped." This is where you to try to instantly shrink yourself to the non-grower's size. Beware of this! Two growth "deaths" do not equal life.

Fortunately, there is a road that heads in the right direction. It is the road marked "Non-attachment." Here, you let the small pieces that do exist in your relationship be just one part of your total life. However, this requires that you let go of how you want your relationship to be and work with what is available. On this road, life beyond your relationship starts catching your attention more than your relationship. But you must be careful that you don't just fill up your time with outside activities. Filling up time doesn't have the same effect as filling your soul.

The imbalance in your relationship will create dissatisfaction if you are counting on that relationship to be your primary source of soul fulfillment. If you can let that attachment go, you can find true satisfaction by setting worthy goals for expression outside your relationship. This not only is a satisfying solution for you, but it takes the pressure of imbalance off your partner.

A worthy goal might be to find a project that focuses on saving the environment. Another possibility might be to get involved in a spiritual group of people who are about bringing more Light and Truth to the world. Just remember, whatever you find that fits your need to be bigger must be more than just a time-filler. While there is nothing wrong with joining a bridge club, for instance, make sure it is not just a time-filler when you are trying to meet the need of making a contribution in life.

Staying attached to your partner being your only source of Sharing, Support and Love is deadly. Even if you both are growing together, attachment to having your partner meet all your needs creates a huge stress on the relationship. A growing relationship can be a great support system, but it can never be your total fulfillment. There is no need to despair if your relationship isn't big; just let it be what it is and step outside to a bigger world.

Stepping outside the boundaries of your relationship can be scary. The fear of loss is sometimes an overwhelming fear. Just keep in mind that losing what you don't have doesn't really hurt at all. In truth, you will be preserving what you really do have by not demanding that the relationship be everything.

Turning Points

It is not uncommon for a "relationship" which has had no help in its evolution to come to a turning point. This is a time when the so-called relationship has made a change for the worse. This is different from having your relationship shrink, age, build up negativity, or change its Love. Turning points occur when the relationship goes from peaceful to spiteful, from exciting to boring, from cooperative to separate, or from lustful to stale. Your relationship may have originally been heading in a good direction, but ended up on a path to destruction.

Turning points are usually stressful for you both, but sometimes they can go unnoticed by one of you. When the stressed-out one says that things will have to change or she or he is leaving, the oblivious one is shocked. However, more often than not, both of you are keenly aware that the road you are traveling is coming to no good end. You simply do not know what to do about it. Somewhere along the line, the relationship got turned around. All too often, help is sought only after one of you has already given up hope, or after you have gone so far down the "bad" road that the damage is irreparable. Sadly, it is then too late.

More than likely, a turning point will not occur if you apply the awareness and tools offered in this book. However, if you are already at a turning point and you haven't passed the destruction line, action needs to be taken. A third person, such as a relationship counselor, can help tremendously, but this person cannot do the everyday relationship work for you. Both of you have to be willing to make the relationship a living entity. Each of you must give up your identity as a person who *has* a relationship and become a person who is willing to *create* one. In other words, you both must be willing to turn around.

It is from this place of new understanding, about the two of you jointly creating a relationship space separate from either of you, that a third entity is able to be birthed. This new definition helps take away the sense of failure when anything goes wrong in the relationship and replaces it with a feeling of freedom. Blame can be given up when guilt is absent. Blame tells you that the direction this relationship has taken is the other person's fault. Under the blame, you have hidden the truth that you are half of the relationship. Thus, owning your part in the turn of events clears the guilt that surrounds the hidden truth and makes it unnecessary to blame your partner. This allows you, as a couple, a bigger space to address problem areas and the freedom to do so.

All too often, couples come to me for help while both of them are pointing a finger at the other. When your finger is pointing at someone else, your other fingers are pointed at you, but rarely are these fingers noticed. In the old paradigm of relationship where each was responsible for the other person, someone had to take the blame if something went wrong. Since no one really wants that blame burden, finger pointing seemed to be the solution.

There are times when I am able to get couples to see the futility in finger pointing, but if it has reached the critical point of intense guilt and blame, then it is almost impossible to build a third entity relationship space.

A turning point in your relationship may even show that a true relationship never existed. Instead, it was only the two of you believing you had a relationship because you gave to each other's needs. If your relationship is built around meeting each other's needs instead of heart energies, there is no possibility of resonance exchange. The best balance that you can hope for is an even checks-and-balance system. That kind of system requires care-taking. You take care of your partner's needs as many times as your partner takes care of yours. It is more like a barter system than a sharing.

I could fill another book with all the needs that people bring to each other to be cared for, so I am just going to list broad areas here. The most common needs that draw couples into a falsc sense of togetherness usually fall into one of these four categories:

1. a cure for loneliness,
2. a fix for sexual hormones,
3. proof that you are desirable, and
4. a desire to meet society's standards.

Coming from any one of these four categories means you can only have an imitation relationship. The most common definition of an imitation relationship is "You give up some parts of yourself and I'll give up some parts of myself, and we will keep some parts for ourselves." Now, compare that to seeing your relationship as a resonating of heart energies in a jointly defined space.

This new definition of a real relationship space ensures that giving and receiving can happen at the same time, in balanced amounts. This eliminates the checks-and-balance system where a mental and emotional record keeps tally of how often you each held up your end of the care-taking deal.

Real relationships are constantly being redefined as the partners grow. Therefore, critical turning points never happen in real relationships. Real relationships are ever-growing, ever-changing entities that express in ways that fit both partners. They do not take away from the individual spaces, but enhance them. The only giving that happens is to a relationship space of resonating heart energies. Thus, giving and receiving happen simultaneously.

This doesn't mean that a real relationship marriage can't evolve into a simple friendship. It can. But a real relationship is a living entity, and while it must continually change shapes, it won't die. You may even choose not to maintain physical contact with someone with whom you birthed a real relationship, but the heart energies you birthed through the initial joining will continue to empower you both as well as the mass consciousness. The energies will live on even if the physical part of the relationship doesn't exist anymore.

Because the picture of relationship this world has handed you is about giving to the other person by doing for them, it is probably hard to think of a relationship as being anything beyond physical interactions. It is this false perception that has created so many hateful divorces. As long as you see material things and shared happenings as the creation of the relationship, instead of energies, you will attach strongly to those physical things and happenings. This is one of the main reasons so many divorce situations focus on demanding a just return of money and property.

When you switch to the new paradigm of an *energy-exchange relationship*, you are no longer putting your energy directly into inanimate physical things. Instead, both energies will go into an agreed-upon relationship definition. As both of you express your heart energy into the agreed-upon physical doing forms, the relationship space gets stronger. The individual spaces also become more because they have synergistically resonated together through the joint intent. Energy has gone from two separate Hearts into an agreed-upon definition to become one. Then physical forms become only vehicles to express your jointly expressed heart energies.

It is this cycle of flow that creates physical manifestation. In other words, you and your partner bring heaven to earth. Energy-exchange relationships give beautiful gifts to the world. Thus, the belongings and money are seen as the outcome of the relationship, not the relationship. Inanimate objects do not contain life in and of themselves. They can only be the outcome of an energy creation.

Once you get comfortable seeing everything in your relationship being about the exchange of heart energies, you will then be able to experience yourself in relationship even while in separate locations. For example, the two of you can define forms together to share the energy of Responsibility while one is at home and one is at work. The energy of Play can be exchanged while one of you plays with the children and the other plays golf. For you to experience an energy exchange relationship, both of you need to be in the same energy and have the intent of connecting. The forms don't need to be the same if the subject is the energy. It is the intent of exchange that makes it so, not the forms or the location.

If you are at a turning point, stop to see what the intent of your relationship has been. Check to see what you each felt you were giving and why you were giving it. If you can back those "givings" into a different subject — an energy of the Heart — then you can begin redefining forms that will cover both of your real expressions. Be forewarned. Unless both of you are willing to make these changes, you had best prepare for some rough times ahead, if not an ending. Even if you fix the immediate problem, you won't be bringing new life. You need to turn around and start over.

Healing Old Wounds

Starting over with a new definition and a new intent does not automatically heal old wounds. Usually someone or something needs to act as a mediator. Relationship counselors are trained to do this. I also have found that such things as writing in a couple's journal or speaking through puppets to one another can also facilitate sharing deep, vulnerable hurts. This type of sharing will need to be for the purpose of clearing, not for the purpose of imposing blame. This means that boundaries around the sharing will need to be set in place beforehand.

Sharing groups are great for opening you up to accepting human frailties — yours and others'. This acceptance is a very important tool to have if you are trying to heal and forgive. The purpose of the group should be to move you beyond your outside attachments that are causing you pain and keeping you victimized, to a realization that you hold power as an energy person. Group support not only helps in times of relationship stress, but can be beneficial to a relationship even when it is going smoothly. A group oftentimes gives you a bigger perspective than you are able to claim by yourself.

Shrinking Spaces

Having an overview helps when you and/or your partner are in a down place, causing the relationship to get small or contract. It is difficult to tell whether the relationship is in a small space or you are. When you are in the middle of an issue, you are contracted and your whole world tends to seem that way. When you are past your issue, and expanded, your relationship may seem bigger than it really is. So when your relationship gets small, how can you tell if it is you or the relationship? Check to see if you are filling (not just completing) your interactions with your defined heart energies. If you aren't, then it is you that has contracted. If you are bringing all that you committed to bring, then your partner is the one who is in a shrinking space.

After you have inspected to see if you are filling your relationship energy containers and found them full, you then need to have a heart-to-heart talk with your partner. Perhaps your partner is going through something personal that needs to be talked about. Perhaps your partner has simply become slack in the relationship commitment. Either way, talking about it may be all it takes. Then again, you may have to redefine some of the relationship forms.

Does temporary shrinking mean you are at a crisis point? It may seem that way, but more than likely it means that your relationship simply needs some temporary adjustment. It is like wearing a belt that makes room for those extra big meals as well as takes up the slack on those lean days. However, redefining is necessary. You can't just say, "It's a phase and it will go away if I leave it alone." Doing nothing will throw your relationship out of balance, which can create an even bigger problem.

What if your partner stays small in the relationship even when the personal crisis is over? You then have a relationship crisis on your hands. You will have to pull some of your energy out, or you will get out of balance. Truth be told, if you must keep defining smaller to bring balance, you will work your way out of the relationship. Having no relationship is better than killing off your own space by giving to a relationship space that is too small. This possibility is so scary that many stop redefining and hang on to their too-small relationship. The only definition they have is one of hope that some day things will turn around.

It helps if the two of you decide ahead of time what too-small looks like. Then you will not be tempted to hold on to the relationship until you start shrinking yourself. Nor will you feel overly rejected if your partner finds it necessary to leave.

To define an ending point ahead of time, you must know what heart energies are necessities for you to share in a relationship. These will be the parts of you that you hold most dear. For example, one of you may need the heart energies of Commitment, Honesty and Persistence in your life all the time. The other may always need the energies of Play, Flexibility, and Spontaneity to be present. Even though, in this example, the two of you might share other heart energies, these six energies must be the foundation stones of your relationship. This means they must at least have a presence. An absence of one or two might be okay for a short period of time. But to have any of them missing for a long time probably will be a signal that the physical part of the relationship is no longer working, and shrinking will inevitably happen.

To stay in a continually shrinking relationship means you will either shrink with it or pull out. Since it is a third entity, a relationship space is a womb for your Heart, a place where the Heart can birth energies, and a shrinking non-functional womb can no longer serve the birthing process. But leaving does not mean the end. It simply means you share what you have birthed and grown up with another relationship where a new womb can be built. You can leave knowing that you not only gifted each other (you take those gifts with you), but you also gifted the planet by empowering the mass consciousness.

Mismatched Heart Energies

There will always be mismatched heart energies in your relationship, but there are ones that are so important to each person that they will need to be continually well-matched if the relationship is going to be successful. All subsidiary, mismatched heart energies can become the responsibility of each individual. The foundation stones are the responsibility of the relationship.

Dark spaces occur in the relationship when you refuse to withdraw your mismatched heart energies. Instead, you keep hoping that if you stay put, your partner will come around and match you. In fact, many people abort a relationship the minute they discover a mismatch. Others slide from hoping into instructing or even demanding. All that these efforts accomplish is to create distance from the energies that really do match. Consider how much time you waste wanting what you don't have when you could be enjoying what you do have.

If you feel as though you are doing all the work in your relationship, then you are either not letting the defined foundation-stone energies be the focus, or you are not being responsible for your own space. There is no light in either approach. No matter how much work you do, you cannot make mismatched energies match.

One of my clients had a run of three one-year relationships. He had many wonderful heart energies. He had Honesty, Loyalty, Caring, and Sharing — all highly desired by the women he dated. However, he had no Commitment and no Love. He had grown up with parents who simply tolerated each other. They both may have had Love and Commitment, but they were too angry to share it. He decided early on that he did not ever want to be married. His image of marriage was one of tolerance, not Love. He had no desire to commit to that life of misery. He was honest, so he told women up front that he did not want to get married. However, they all thought if they were wonderful enough, they could make him change his mind. None would accept that Commitment or Love were simply not energies he possessed. This focus on what he lacked naturally caused stress in all his relationships.

Unfortunately, he attracted women who, like his mother, had Commitment and Love as foundation stones to their being. With no match available for their special energies, they would become very unhappy, even though neither of these energies was listed on his Heart resume. That fact was forgotten, and misery became the focus. After we separated his mother's and father's mismatched energies, and saw them as separate people, he was then able to claim a relationship that matched some of his foundation energies.

It was so sad to me that these wonderful people (the man and all three of his women) were programmed in their childhoods to have mismatched relationships. If that is your programming, you will need to do as my client did and separate who each parent was from the image you had of them together. None of the three women were willing to believe the mismatches had anything to do with their programming. Instead, they preferred to point fingers at the man, just before moving on to the next mismatched relationship.

Before you can make a match, you must first take personal responsibility for the energies you possess. Then you need to decide which ones are foundation stones for you in a relationship, and start looking for those energies as you try on relationships. If you are in a relationship already, be willing to discover if those energies exist in a different shape from yours. Without laying the ground work, you will fall into the traditional trap of making your partner responsible for matching what can't be matched. Mismatched heart energies make mismatched relationships.

The act of sex can be sacred
only if two spiritual Hearts
are manifesting through
pure mental and emotional channels.

Sacred Sex

13

While hints on how to be more sensual or spontaneous sexually can be beneficial, they can't help you achieve the deep satisfaction that spiritual resonance does. It is the merging of two people's energies into one that takes a couple to new heights.

The physical is the place of manifestation. It is the place where you act out who you are spiritually, as defined by your mind and perceived by your emotions. Thus, the act of sex can be sacred only if two spiritual Hearts are manifesting through pure mental and emotional channels. Let's say that your Heart wants to manifest Passion through the sex act, but your mind has defined Passion in a limited way, and your emotions perceive too much Passion putting you dangerously out of control. Since heart energies have to pass through the mind and the feelings in order to express physically, how pure is the heart energy of Passion going to be when it expresses through the form of sex while one or both are in resistance?

Just telling yourself that you are going to feel differently or think in a new way does not make it happen. You literally have to let go of your old ways of thinking and feeling and replace them with new energy constructs. In other words, you must let the heart energy of Passion create its own space in your mind and feelings. Once your thoughts and feelings open to newness, the Heart can then express itself the way it wants to without clutter (such as your mother's internal voice) getting in the way.

Unfortunately, you can't take the latest magazine article on sexual freedom and create a fantasy of a "new and freer you" unless you make an internal space for that to happen. After you have identified the voices and feelings inside that resist the newness of the Heart, tell them to leave and go back where they came from. Then you will have space inside you for new images and textures. You will be able to discover fully the size of your heart energy of Passion and what shapes it wants to take. You may discover that it is different from what the magazines have told you it should be. In other words, you may not fit the media's sexual image at all. This does not make you odd or non-sexual. In fact, you can have very little Passion, and still be a sexy person. You may find that Spontaneity or Sensitivity is just as sexy as Passion. By looking inside to see what parts of you want to express sexually, you may find something totally different from what the movies tell you it should be. Your sexually expressed heart energy may even be something very gentle, such as Kindness, which is at the opposite end of the intensity spectrum from Passion.

Sex does not have to be about any one expression. It can be about Sharing, Play, Adventure, or even Safety, to name a few of the Heart's possible character traits that can enjoy sex. The greatest offense to your sexuality is the one brought by the outside that tells you how you are to be sexually. Isn't it true you have been shown by the media what sexy looks like, sounds like, and even feels like? Does it ever mention who is to be expressing through those prescribed forms? The answer is a resounding NO! The real essence of people is not included in the subject of sex. Unfortunately, sex has been described as something you do instead of an expression of who you are.

The public image of sex is so "canned" that very little room is left for personal sacredness. Sex is presented as an act of external stimulation for the purpose of creating wonderful internal results. You are told that if you are sexy enough, the opposite gender will adore and love you. And, in addition to good looks, you must perform all the required external stimulation in the best possible ways.

Sacred sex does not do away with external stimulation. It simply directs sex actions so that they are in alignment with the instructions that come with a specific heart energy. For example, if you are a person of great Gentleness, that energy may well be part of your sexual expression. It may prefer to express through light caressing of the whole body rather than being focused on intense stimulation of the genital area.

To have sacred sex, you have to honor what is sacred in each of you. The heart energies that each of you has available to bring to the love-making act must be honored and included. This doesn't mean you can't verbally express to your partner what you physically need to be sexually satisfied. Just be sure to do so with an energy name attached. For example, you might say, "Please massage my thighs in an Honoring way."

Let's say a Kindness energy person gets together with a person of intense Passion. The Kindness person has heretofore chosen gentle forms, and the Passion person has always preferred intensity. More than likely, both will verbally share what forms they need physically, which is fine. However, they both must realize that all heart energies have a full scale of expression. And perhaps their Hearts have created an opportunity to explore new dimensions of Kindness and Passion.

Gentle heart energies can be intense without being rough. Strong heart energies can be gentle without being weak. Oftentimes we choose a partner who expresses heart energies on the opposite end of the intensity scale from us in order to stretch us a bit in our expression.

You don't have to be like someone in order to cover them in intensity. Everyone needs to be strong and soft, powerful and vulnerable, gentle and intense — and all heart energies have the capacity to cover from one end of the volume scale to the other.

To honor who you are, you must stay within the parameters of your specific heart energies. In other words, you may not be Courage, Focus, and Strength. But you may be Compassion, Health, and Sincerity. Honor who you are and don't plagiarize someone else. In addition, you must give each of your individual heart energies permission to have its full range of expression. This desire to expand your Heart will override many of your mind's objections and your emotion's resistance to new forms of expression.

If your old belief system says that Kindness must be gentle and Passion must be intense, then you are limiting your Heart and theirs. If you believe one heart energy to be a better fit in the act of sex than another, then you once again are limiting yourself. Sacred sex is simply about bringing together you and your partner's essence to the space marked "sex" in your relationship. It requires finding forms that fit together for both of you and then being willing to expand your expression range to fill those forms.

The satisfaction that comes from merging deeper into spiritual resonance with another person far surpasses the selfish space of just being physically satisfied. To fall into society's version of sexual intimacy means giving up the chance to have sacred sex. Sacred sex isn't the glue that bonds a relationship. Instead, it is the result of a bonded relationship. It is the manifestation of all the work you have put into defining, empowering, and keeping clear your relationship space. Sacred sex is an act of joining that expresses the unity that already exists.

Yes, you may need to try out new sexual expression forms on a continual basis as your relationship grows, but you will never again need to go back to selfish, self-satisfying sex, or sex canned by the media. Instead, you will discover how to take heart resonance to a more exalted place. Connectedness will be your intent. Sacredness will be your result.

Personal Preparedness for Sex

While some people eat raw oysters or take DHEA to prepare for sex, others look at pictures of nude models and watch sex flicks. Sexual chemistry has become so overrated that you might wonder what is wrong with you if you aren't "turned on" all the time.

To prepare for sex, you certainly need to make sure your mind and emotions are clutter-free, with all worries and distractions put aside. There is no way to be a pure channel for heart energies unless you are totally present in the now. Clutter-free also means that you have released any judgments about sex being naughty or bad and replaced those thoughts with new truths about its potential for bringing sacredness into your relationship. Clutter-free also means you have let go of all feelings of inferiority about your looks and performance and replaced those feelings with anticipation about getting to share realness.

Sacredness does not mean that you can't think, feel or look sexy. Energy cannot carry the Heart's intent into physical action without the participation of all parts of you. As a matter of fact, you will think, feel, and look sexier than ever before when you allow any one of your heart energies to define itself in sexual expression.

As I said earlier, one of the biggest and most difficult hurdles to overcome on your journey to sacred sex is perceiving sex to be different from the Hollywood version. In fact, a good preparation exercise is to take any heart energy that doesn't fit the movie screen image and fantasize how it can express through a sexual joining. Actually, this kind of fantasizing should happen often so that you won't get caught in the small expression of the same heart energy every time you have sex. For sex to be sacred, all parts of you should have a space to express sexually if they so desire.

Since relationship sex employs the participation of another person, you must take an inventory of that relationship before you are ready to have sex. A relationship space needs to reach a certain standard of quality before a sacred joining can happen in the physical. However, there is never a fixed reading. You may have a beautiful sacred space one day and have it get cluttered and contaminated the next. Preparing for sacred sex with another person goes way beyond just being "turned on." Having sex just because you are turned on would be like jumping into water to swim every time you see water. Needless to say, that would not be appropriate or desirable because the location, time, and preparedness aren't in place. The same parameters hold true for sex. The time, place and preparedness need to be in place for it to be a sacred expression.

Not only do both of you need to be ready personally, but your relationship space must be ready as well. This means that you both need to be Heart-centered with agreed-upon definitions and forms in place. Don't worry; spontaneity isn't left out of this formula. It takes only a few seconds of time to check in with your "awareness meter" to see if you and your partner are in a clear space. If you know your partner well enough to be having sex, then you know his or her dominant heart energies. You may not have talked about forms, but sighs and body movements say a lot in directing you to forms that will work as expression vehicles. The main thing is to be connected at the Heart, and all else will work out with ease.

Since all heart energies must find physical expression in order to be complete, finding a balance of forms is of primary importance. Sex is a wonderful, beautiful form to add to the mix of physical expression if both of you are physically capable of having genital sex. However, you or your partner may not always be capable of having sex in a genital way, or one might not like to have it as often as the other person. In such cases, you need to transfer the energies you would like to express sexually —with the same intensity — to other forms.

A client of mine entered male menopause and not only lost all ability to have an erection but also lost all interest in sex. Needless to say, his wife felt both angry and rejected for awhile.

Thankfully, she had been on a spiritual growth path for a few years and knew that she was never a victim of someone else's creation — even her partner's! Rather than shut down all sexual feelings or have an affair, she set about trying to discover what combinations of heart energies, and to what intensity, she had been expressing through the form of sex. She was then able to transfer those energies to other activities. Some expressions became hers alone and some stayed in the relationship space, but with different forms.

Creativity was one of her most powerful sexual expressers, supported mostly by Spontaneity. Her next, less prominent, expressers were Love and Honor. She divided these into two categories. She started her own business that stretched her Creativity beyond its previously known boundaries — but not to the breaking point. All the decisions that go along with starting a new business used up what leftover Spontaneity she had. The two lesser energies of Love and Honor shaped into new forms of relationship expression with her husband.

This example points out that sex is just one more form of expression in a relationship. It is not the foundation, as you have oftentimes been told. However, sex can be a very intimate interaction in which you and your partner can engage. It should never get boring or commonplace. It should not be shelved for lack of value or worn out from overuse. Be careful not to let the routine of everyday affairs and the rushing to and fro to accomplish your to-do list become enemies of your sexual sacredness. Neither should you let sexual addictions replace sacredness. Fortunately, none of these things will happen when you personally prepare for the sacredness of sex before each sexual encounter.

Fighting and Sex

It may seem strange to put fighting and sex together since they are at opposite ends of the scale in physical relationship expression. Yet they both are symbolic anchors to keep the relationship space from shrinking to a small margin in the middle. Sex is seen symbolically as a form for merging two energies into a common whole. Fighting, on the other hand, is the symbol for separation. Actually, in healthy relationships, both are needed — merging and separating. This doesn't mean that you must have sex to join, or fight in order to discover your separate spaces, but discovering of both needs to happen, and sex and fighting are possible sources. Since the most common forms for recognizing the boundaries of a relationship are sex and fighting, you need to be aware of the purpose both can serve.

I have stressed the importance of joining energies in your relationship. Without this anchor at one end of your relationship space, life together will become a series of robotic interactions with a few sporadic connections. Similarly, without the disagreements (or fighting) to anchor the relationship on the other end, of problem awareness, your relationship will become the same thing — a series of robotic interactions with a few sporadic connections.

Fighting usually centers on a problem that needs to be solved. That is a good thing if it takes both of you into your separate spaces to see what isn't working for you individually. However, it is a detrimental thing if the problem is seen as solely the fault of the other person. Even if the other person comes around to your demands and the problem seems to be solved, no new boundary of energies has been created. You have to go inward to see what you need. Your partner must do the same and then you can come back together and solve the problem. Using this method means that an extension of the previous relationship boundary has been created — more Heart has been added with a new definition.

If the anchor is too heavy on either end — connecting or fighting — then much is lost. Trying to connect constantly without a reality check as to what is not working will drain the zest out of the most compatible of partnerships. On the other hand, fighting all the time, without the consummation of Hearts connecting, also will strangle a relationship. As with all things, balance must be maintained. For connectedness to stay alive there must be a periodic separation so that personal inventories can be made.

To let fighting get out of balance means you are reinforcing the problem rather than using it to find the cure. Every time an argument gets prolonged, the unconscious is fed more negative food about your partner and the relationship. The unconscious soon comes to believe that basically your partner is hopelessly incompetent, stubborn, and/or selfish. And, even if you are sure you are right and they are wrong, you will feel like a powerless victim when you can't change your partner. These images, unless destroyed, get added to your room of other negative images. All of this gets stored away in your unconscious mind. Pretty soon you have more material on what is wrong with your relationship than what is right about it.

Fighting should be a win-win situation. It should be seen as the "lie detector" that points out non-heartful spaces in the relationship. It can let you know that a form needs to be tweaked or changed altogether. It is essential, however, for both of you to have a voice in the "fight." Without two equal fighters, there is always a bully and a victim. These two players can never move towards the middle. Instead, they must hold up separate sides of the issue all by themselves or give in. There can be no win-win. There can only be two losers.

After both of you express your discontent — which may range from very loud to mildly intense — it is time to start taking the focus off of the physical problem and turn to see what new heart energy both of you want to express in the troubled situation. Once the focus is shifted from the physical problem to the energy need, the "fight" is on its way to resolution. Finding compatible forms may still present some difficulty, but no longer are you working from the stalemate position of one being right and the other being wrong.

Fighting should never escalate to physical damage of people or things. Usually it doesn't, with couples who carry the intent and the tools to create a real relationship. Still, there are moments in every relationship when someone gets really mad. This is especially true with extremely passionate people. The key is not to get pulled into the other person's space. Remember, fighting requires short-term separation. From the vantage point of your space, you will be able to tell if the fight is getting out of balance. You also can find safety in your own space. From your space you will have the clarity to know how to handle the situation. This may require that you leave the room or even the house until your partner's rage has been pulled back into his or her own space. If you are the enraged one, you also can leave the battle ground.

You can come back to partnership when the anger and hurt (or other emotions) coming up are no longer the primary subject. Emotions can be present and even look quite nasty and still not be the main intent of the conversation. Until both of you are ready to move through the anger to get to the real subject (the heart energies wanting to express) you are not ready to discuss the problem together. Until partnership is possible, it is still a personal problem.

Learning to "fight" well is of key importance in maintaining a growing, healthy relationship. It is unfortunate that most fighting is just about dumping a lot of emotion on the other person with the intent to make that person change so you can feel better. Good fighting means equal positions of rightness and a large measure of giving up attachments. To allow for equality and to release attachments, you must be willing to go into your personal space and take an inventory of what is old and what is new. Then throw away what is old and isn't needed and go back to your partner to create together what is new and is presently needed.

Many times, giving up an attachment means you have to say, "Perhaps my way is not the only way." Or sometimes it may even mean saying, "I am sorry my patterns hurt you." Movement is always the theme. Even "good" attachments must be given up if they are blocks to energy movement. None of these evaluations can happen while you are still angry — so get through it first. Write, take a walk, or beat on a pillow — whatever it takes — but get through it so you're headed in the direction of your clear space.

Correct fighting takes you to heart connections. Heart connections cause growth which creates stress that leads back to fighting. To try to stay in the middle only makes the relationship shrink and become stagnant.

To be considered extended family,
the "outsider" must possess
one of the defined heart energies
of the relationship
and be willing to share it
with both of you equally.

The Extended Family

14

Establishing relationships with extended family can be enriching or depleting to your primary relationship, depending on how you set it up. It would be rather "Pollyanna-ish" to assume that all your relationship associations are perfect. Usually there are some good ones thrown in with the not-so-good ones. Then, within the good ones, there are those that reach extended family status and those that don't.

Every person your relationship interacts with on a regular basis can be considered extended family, in that they give your relationship a chance to extend its heart space synergistically. However, this must be done correctly, or "outsiders" can impact your relationship negatively. Extending your relationship space synergistically means you are willing to join at least one of your relationship heart energies with someone outside your twosome. This may be children, blood relatives, neighbors, work associates, or a longtime friend of yours or your partner's.

Just because you have known someone since high school doesn't mean the person is automatically part of your extended relationship. You can have friends that your partner likes, and vice versa, but these friends may not necessarily make it to the extended family list. To make that list, the "outsider" must possess one of the defined heart energies of the relationship and be willing to share it with both of you equally. This doesn't mean that he or she spends exactly the same time with each of you. It simply means that there is a willingness to share with the two of you equally.

In order for "outsiders" to become extended family, they must know how to relate to a relationship. This gets tricky if they have never had a real relationship, because more than likely they will try to relate to you and your partner's individual spaces. It then becomes the responsibility of both you and your partner to keep them focused on the "our" space. An example of this would be dealing with your partner's child from a previous marriage as a parental unit. At first, the child will relate solely with the blood parent because that is what they know; however, the child can learn to relate differently as he or she becomes acquainted with this new third "person."

All too often, relationship partners have their own special friends, and then together they attend other couple or family gatherings. This is not the extended family of the Heart. Even being blood-related does not make them extended family. Your relationship, as a third entity, has the ability to resonate with the Hearts of others just the same as you do individually. Resonating always empowers all concerned in the heart connection. Therefore, it is growthful for your relationship to extend itself to others.

This is a difficult concept, so let's look at some real life examples. Sam rides to work with George and plays golf with him on weekends. They share common interests but they also share the heart energies of Support and Play through those common interests. Support is one of the foundation heart energies of Sam and Suzie's relationship, but it is not one of George and Ginny's. It is a bit awkward inviting George over and not Ginny, so does that mean George is never going to make the extended family list?

In this example, a strong resonance may exist with George and the Sam-and-Suzie relationship. This doesn't mean that whatever heart energies Ginny brings can't be appreciated and enjoyed by both Sam and Suzie; they can. Ginny can be a guest to the relationship at the same time George is a family contributor. If you didn't get lost in the semantics of this example, you can see that some people, while enjoyable associates, contribute little to empower the relationship, while others bring much, even if both people seem to interact in the same ways.

Making the distinction between friendly associations and family contributors will help you in scheduling your relationship's social calendar. While it is fine for you and your partner to have your own friends, you must be careful not to neglect the relationship. It needs friends, too.

In-laws or "Out-laws"

Some families have such strong family patterns that every single member gets "outfitted" in the same way. I know one man who grew up in a very strict religious group. All his family believed, dressed, acted and interacted in accordance with that particular faith. While this was not the type of extended family I am talking about, they certainly believed themselves to be a supportive unit. Then, one day, this man (I'll call him Gerald) decided to step outside the family patterns. He started reading literature and listening to tapes of other thinking and acting modes. All at once he became an outsider because he gave up his family's shared patterns.

When Gerald started expressing his heart energies of Growth, Expansion and Courage, he drew to himself other people who were able to resonate those energies with him. He gave up a family of sameness to have a diverse family of the Heart. He was able to develop relationships that empowered who he was, rather than just make him comfortable about his patterns. He still visited his blood relatives, but they had become acquaintances, not extended family.

Families based on common patterns of behavior and beliefs may get along well, but they do not necessarily resonate with a heart energy that supports the relationship. On the other hand, families can grow away from the common patterns of childhood into diverse patterns and still be able to relate well, if they bring a realness that reaches beyond sameness.

The unfortunate tale that even enlightened couples often tell is that they go home to their blood families and try to become who they used to be when they were growing up. They may seem to still be part of the family, but in reality they are miserable in their charade. On the other hand, flaunting your differences is not the answer either. You must simply change the focus to the energy or energies that you can share or at least appreciate. Having done this, you are able to look beyond the patterns to a point of connection.

Let's look at another example. Juanita's sister-in-law was arrogant, selfish, and small-minded. Needless to say, Juanita had no desire to emulate those patterns, nor could she find any heart energies to relate to. A stand-off would have been a good solution, except Juanita loved her brother. Even though the brother was also pretty restricted in his realness, he did have some Love to share. In order for Juanita to make him part of her extended family, she had to set boundaries around the aggravating patterns of both her brother and sister-in-law. By making large portions of their interactions off-limits, she could still enjoy the Love space that she and her brother shared.

Now the sister-in-law was another matter. No relationship was possible there because they shared no heart energies. So even though Juanita had to talk with the sister-in-law about such things as food provisions when the families got together, she didn't interact beyond the mundane. This worked for Juanita's personal space, but what about the relationship space she and her husband shared? Juanita's husband had Love, but it was a totally different shape from her brother's. Therefore, true sharing from Juanita and her husband's relationship wasn't possible. This didn't mean they couldn't be polite around one another. However, it did mean that Juanita had to be careful not to take away from her marriage relationship by spending lots of time with her brother.

This brings up another important point. Love, Loyalty, Commitment, Support, etc., can carry the same name and be very different in content. While Juanita's Love was big enough to cover both her husband's Love and her brother's, neither the brother nor the husband could relate to each other through their separate types of Love. While no two people will ever be exactly alike, there must always be a point of similarity for the two to join. It was important for Juanita to express both types of Love, but she also had a responsibility not to ignore her relationship when all three people got together. Keeping an internal balance, by making sure all parts of your Heart have external expression, and keeping an external balance, by making sure no one relationship overrides another, are both important and sometimes difficult.

Besides the internal and external balancing in the Juanita story, there is the one-on-one balancing that must be addressed. The story of John's mother should help. John's mother was a very generous woman. She could hardly wait until she had a daughter-in-law to give to. When the day arrived, she was dismayed to discover her new daughter-in-law, while loving and kind, was not very good at receiving. John's mother had to give up her image of what having a daughter-in-law would look like and re-group. Fortunately, she was able to do so. She stopped trying to bring gifts and started finding ways they could just be kind to each other. She conquered the one-on-one balancing act.

Most "out-law" situations can be turned around with the right intent and a lot of insight. But without the right tools, perfectly good in-laws get labeled "out-laws." Remember, a marriage is more than just adding a spouse to the family. It also brings a relationship. The foundation stones of who you are individually may not be the same as the ones that make up your relationship. You literally have brought two strangers — your mate and your relationship — with whom your blood family must learn how to interact. You probably have told them a lot about your new partner, but this unknown third entity called a relationship will be all new to them. So be patient and let the introductions start small.

All too often, the "married-in" partner sits back and tries to be polite and pleasant while visiting the in-laws, and that is as good as it ever gets. It is sad but true that few relationships get to be empowered by the original family units because they never get properly introduced. Acceptance is good, but it doesn't come close to resonance. To get beyond polite, you have to be willing to put yourself out there. Even though the defining may not be as deliberate with the in-laws as it is with your partner, you are still doing it as you try out different patterns when expressing yourself as a relationship unit.

Even though John's mother was able to develop a genuine relationship with her daughter-in-law, she still held her son in the same relationship definition they had before the marriage. That meant she had a relationship with John and with John's wife, but none with their relationship entity.

Your Kids, My Kids, and Our Kids

When children get transferred from one parent to another, it is essential that the adults have a clear picture of their marriage. By that I mean they need to have their feet firmly planted in which heart energies bond them together and what forms they are going to express them through. Every decision made by the new parents regarding the children must be made in light of who they are as a unit. For one parent to step outside the relationship in dealing with a child's issues means the child has only one parent. Not only will the partner have no place in the family, but the couple's relationship won't either.

Many times, divorcés carry guilt about breaking up their children's home. Trying to make it up to them is not only destructive for the children, but is also destructive for any intimate relationship you may have. The best course of action is to stop trying to be a super parent in the over-giving way, and instead offer them an opportunity to resonate in a bigger way. As in the case of the in-laws, the children need to get acquainted with the relationship entity as well as the new partner. This takes time, patience, and effort. It can be very rewarding, but it rarely happens instantly.

Furthermore, you cannot expect your new relationship as a couple to get the same response that your old relationship did, so don't compare. It does not have the exact same composition, so how could it get the same response? If you compare, you can be sure the children will also. There may be heart energies that are similar, but even the same energy of Support, for example, may come in different shapes. When unfair comparisons come up short, they are often justified by the statement, "Love will grow." That kind of thinking traps you in a prison of the future. People either have the heart energy of Love or they don't. However, it may take time for all the qualities of that Love to be defined and expressed.

Start small in presenting your new relationship to the children. Not slow, but small. Show the children who the two of you are together, a piece at a time. Then, do not let their response be the judge of that piece's value. After all, they will be dealing with all this newness in the best way they can, and the best may have lots of fear or anger in the mix. In other words, their actions may not equal the correctness of the Ingalls children in *Little House on the Prairie*. Just keep in mind they will not know how to do this relationship stuff unless they are taught.

All families have more than one relationship going on at the same time. Each person has a one-on-one relationship with everyone in the family as well as with the family itself. All of these units are important. However, the couple's relationship should hold the most power in dealing with the children, or the kids will learn well how to play one against the other. It will be by relating to the parents as a couple that the children will come to understand the third entity concept of relationship. This schooling will determine to a large degree the success or failure of their relationships as adults.

*To make decisions about your relationship needs,
you must ask what will serve us both equally,
as well as how much money is available to cover
each of the four areas —
physical, emotional, mental and spiritual.*

Relationship Money

15

Who owns the money? Ownership of the relationship money must be an equal thing or it can't belong to the relationship. However, both of your earnings do not have to go into a common "kitty." Nor do both of you need to earn the same amount of money. In fact, one of you may stay at home and earn no money. Working out the details of how much money is needed for the relationship and which one is going to supply that money, while at the same time keeping ownership equal, are important issues that need to be addressed.

First, you will need to decide together how much money you really need for the relationship. The key word here is "need." It is all too easy to get caught up in the "wants." Defining from the "wants" will end up in financial tension and relationship problems. To make decisions about your relationship needs, you will have to cover all four parts of the relationship — physical, emotional, mental and spiritual. In each of the four areas, you must ask what will serve us both equally, as well as how much money is available to cover each of the four areas.

THE BASIC NEEDS

Relationship needs are really pretty basic. You will physically need housing, food, transportation, clothing, exercise and medical attention. If money is short, you may need to think outside of the box. For example, you might look at two options around housing. You could go for a small apartment or you could opt for a house that could accommodate roommates. While exercise is a must, the financial support required may be as simple as a good pair of walking shoes.

Transportation can get tricky in considering your physical needs. Living in a city where public transportation is available gives people more choices than living in a small town. However, carpooling should always be a possibility to consider. It not only supports you financially, but it supports the environment as well. Convenience is nice, but money availability must come first. Just remember, to spend more than you earn brings total imbalance to your flow and will affect the giving and receiving cycle in all areas of your life.

Medical expenses are often forgotten about until an emergency arises for which you are not prepared. It is always nice to have medical insurance, but it is beyond the financial limits of many couples. If you fit into this latter category, look in advance for doctors that charge less for patients without insurance. Another well-defined plan to cover medical within a tight budget is to eat only healthy food. A steady diet of fresh fruits and vegetables is much cheaper than an illness. In fact it is even cheaper than junk food. Add to your good diet periodic massages and chiropractic, if you can, to help relieve the stress level of your body. Daily stress takes a much larger toll on your body's health than you usually admit.

It is good to decide first what items of clothing you each need to carry out your daily tasks. Add in the few extras needed for special occasions, and you have your basic clothing needs. How many items your basic needs list contains, and how much you spend on them, will depend on the amount of money available. A family with lots of money may have two pages of basic needs clothing listed, while a less wealthy family may have to cut it down to five items. Remember, you can be creative in financially meeting basic needs no matter what size list you have. I knew a lady who always looked as if she had just walked off the pages of a fashion magazine, yet her clothing budget was tiny. She had learned to take her good taste to consignment stores. She had also learned to mix and match as well as discovered the magic of accessorizing. On the other hand, I also knew a lady who spent $400 a month on clothing. She also looked nice.

What was important was that both stayed within the agreed-upon limits of their relationship's financial definition.

Emotionally, your needs may not require much money, but they need to be included. Play, Cleanliness, Order, Beauty and Comfort all keep the emotional climate of a relationship healthy. For instance, coming home to find your home tidy with some items sitting around that please you can do much to lighten the emotional load of the day. Covering your emotions ahead of time in your financial budget eliminates emotional binging with your money later.

The subtle stress created in a relationship by disorder is much greater than most people imagine. Having to hunt for something before you go to work can take ten minutes out of an already tight schedule — not a good beginning. Coming into a messy kitchen when it is time to eat is another subtle stress that can wipe out a good mood in just a matter of minutes. Buying some storage or organizing items, or even budgeting for someone to come clean your house, are certainly things to consider under emotional money spending.

You know well that all work and no play will throw a relationship out of balance. Yet, often recreation is thought of as a spontaneous happening. While the recreation, or Play, of the relationship doesn't need to be overly structured, it does need to be defined. Together you need to outline what activities can represent the heart energy of Play for both of you within the boundaries of the money allotted. Recreation doesn't have to mean going out to expensive restaurants and concerts. It can mean playing a board game after supper every night, putting a puzzle together periodically, inviting company over for dinner once a month, or watching a movie at home while munching popcorn.

You will need to set aside some money to stimulate, enrich and expand your mind. This may be as simple as subscribing to *National Geographic* magazine, going to classes, or surfing the Internet together. Whatever the choices, they must serve you both equally. I have known couples who religiously worked the Sunday newspaper's crossword puzzle to join in a mental activity. Others read books they can discuss together, while some discuss current events with great fervor. Designing a flower garden together can be a great mental sharing. Besides, it will allow you to "kill two birds with one stone." You will not only get to join two great minds, but you will also save money by not needing to hire a landscape architect.

The spiritual area is often overlooked or left as the last area to be considered. It cannot be left out. Even if going to church is listed as your only item in the spiritual, you still must allow money for this area, because money creates flow. And of all the areas your relationship covers, the spiritual needs the most flow. Without a flowing, growing spiritual part to your relationship, it will lose all its purpose and vitality. Giving money to what feeds your relationship Heart helps it to maintain the giving and receiving balance necessary to stay alive.

It is important that the two of you look inside to see what aspects of spirituality help you to recognize the God within and to see life as sacred. It will be a composite of these aspects that you will need to claim for your relationship. Too often, people put the largest percentage of their joint income into their housing and the least into what supports them spiritually. That is sad, because while a nice house is a pleasant accessory, it isn't the life blood of the relationship as is spirituality.

The church may or may not work for both of you as one of the tools for heartful living. Do not fall into the old-time belief that religion and spirituality are one and the same. They are not! Many churches have spiritual people in them, but that doesn't necessarily make the church spiritual. If church is a form chosen by you both, select one carefully, but be open to other spiritual supports as well.

Open your minds to experience alternative spiritual activities, such as yoga or meditation. Self-actualization groups have brought life back to many relationships and have provided on-going vitality to others. There are also many books and audio recordings out there by very enlightened people. Invest your money wisely because your investments in the spiritual will be the most important ones your relationship can make.

Ownership

Oftentimes the person in the relationship who brings home the most money feels ownership of it. While it is healthy for both persons to have money of their own to spend (according to their personal definitions), relationship money must be an "our" thing. Money ownership will tip the balance scale of power in the relationship and create a less-than/greater-than atmosphere.

It is rare for both people of the relationship to make the same amount of money. However, if money is viewed as an energy exchange item, then a balance of energy brought into the relationship can happen. For example, when there is a stay-at-home parent with no income, that partner will need to contribute energy in another way. He or she might bring energy by any number of acts, such as cooking, cleaning, doing the accounting, taking care of the children, caring for the clothes, maintaining the yard, or gardening. All of these activities would cost money if an outsider performed them. Find the going rate and consider the stay-at-home activities as money earned.

All money designated as relationship money must be jointly owned. This doesn't mean that both people must have the same amount of money to spend on themselves. However, too much variance can become a problem if it isn't balanced in another way. Take the example of Josie and Harold. Harold has a job that pays well. Josie's job fits her interests extremely well, but it doesn't pay very much. Harold spends his money on golf and rebuilding vintage cars. Josie had no extra money for hobbies or recreation, so she wanted Harold to do more fun things with her, using relationship money. This got to be such a big source of resentment that Harold started lying about his extra activities. Since Harold was now resentful of any play he had to do with Josie, she got no return from what things they did do together.

A crisis point was about to be reached. Instead of continuing their ongoing escalation of tension, they sat down and worked out a solution. Josie discovered that she could invite her friends over to play games and have just as much fun as Harold did playing golf. Harold generously agreed to pay Josie $10 for every $100 he spent on his antique cars. Josie spent the money in consignment shops where she not only found terrific clothes but got to experience the thrill of finding a really great deal.

Had Harold split all of his money with Josie, he, understandably, would have felt ownership, Josie would have given up her sense of equality, and the division of power would have become lopsided. This happens all too often when couples fall into the old paradigm of relationship that says "If you are married you must share everything." Since the relationship space is fed from the individual spaces, these spaces must not be ignored.

Sharing everything in the relationship space is commonly considered the perfect relationship. Sharing is good, but having no personal spaces is sure death. When you give yourself away, there is nothing left to bring to the relationship. Remember, a relationship space is created by two people giving to it. Two people do not automatically become a relationship space.

Mine and Ours

How much money should become ours and how much should I keep for myself is a frequently asked question. The desire for a big house and a new car often gets put at the top of the relationship list, and then every cent both people earn must be poured into those budgeted slots. This is fine, as long as the energy the relationship receives from the house and car is equal to the amount of energy (money) put into them, and the small amount left over is enough for both partners to meet their individual needs.

The relationship has energy exchange needs and so does each of the partners. To discover which of these needs are real, all of the supposed needs must be identified and have price tags attached. Then you are ready for the sorting to begin. Priorities have to be itemized, and the balance of energy input and output must be measured. You cannot spend more than you make. Neither can you leave out real needs. However, the forms those needs manifest into can take many shapes.

Many supposed needs are not real — they are just forms. Real needs are always backed with a heart energy. For example, you may think you need every room in your house furnished, when in fact you need Comfort and Beauty. Having every room furnished could bring Beauty and Comfort, but so could a beautiful sofa and a supportive mattress.

After both of you have prioritized your real needs, see how many of them are similar enough to become relationship needs. Put price tags on them, and see if you can jointly contribute enough money to cover the whole list. It helps to write down all the forms that you once thought were real needs, but were only emotional attachments. Take this "attachment list" and tear it up, burn it, or crumple it into a little wad. Any action you can take to destroy your "attachment list" will help your unconscious know that it isn't important any more.

After you have prioritized, priced, detached and sorted again, you should be able to come to a workable budget. This process of elimination and choice can happen for the two of you only after you have gone through this process for your personal needs first. If you both don't act responsibly by taking care of your personal needs financially, then your relationship needs will be financially unstable.

Usually a "leakage" happens from one space to another when all three (yours, hers or his, and ours) are not defined correctly. This "leakage" will allow both the area of needs and money to get out of balance. Lack of balance can cause the whole three-space structure to collapse. I wouldn't say that money is the root of all evil as I have sometimes heard. But I would say that improper defining around money can cause a dark spot of tension in a relationship.

Where Does Support Stop and Caretaking Begin?

While it is true that each of you must be responsible for your part in the energy contribution, it is also true that energy (either in the form of tasks or money) is not always constant. There will be times when you need to step outside a definition and lend a helping hand to your partner. The question is not if, but how much and how long.

The "how much" answer has two sides. You cannot deplete your own physical, emotional, mental, spiritual or financial reserves. Neither can you deplete others' belief that they can create for themselves. It is not an act of Kindness or Support to allow your partner to become dependent on you. It is extremely difficult for an adult to claim personal Power and at the same time depend on someone to continually pull them out of financial difficulties. The key word here is continually. Everyone has down times. If not financial, it might be physical, emotional, mental, or spiritual. However, for you to be continually down in any one area, means you have not claimed your Power in that area. When that is true, the best support that can be offered may be a suggestion for professional help.

To cross the line into the too-much help zone means that you have not only weakened your partner's Power but yours as well. Any time you are giving too much in any area, you will become out of balance in your flow of energy. You cannot continually flow outward without a balanced return and stay energetically powerful. Strength and Power happen only at center point — the point of balance.

How long you will offer help should be decided at the beginning of the offer. If you let your partner's need decide how long you will give financial support, you have created an open-ended energy container. In other words, you are not defining closure, but instead you are allowing the other person's need to do the defining. Have you ever given someone, or even yourself, a task with no time limit on it? Usually it doesn't get done or it takes longer than it would have if you had said, "I need this to be finished by so-and-so time." The same is true when lending a financial hand. You need to be in charge of the time limit.

In order to set a time limit that fits you, you must know yourself well. Are you an over-giver or do you lack Generosity? Whichever position you hold, you need to acknowledge it with complete honesty. Then, describe what you perceive to be the opposite end of that spectrum. If you are overly generous, then imagine what it would be like to be stingy. If you lack Generosity, then imagine yourself generous. When you have the whole picture, position yourself in the middle. Middle won't be totally comfortable, but it will be healthier. Letting the other person's need define the situation means leaving yourself out. A relationship does not exist when one of the two is left out.

Another support that you can offer or ask for is temporarily to redefine your financial relationship agreement. Let's say you agreed to pay X amount for restaurant eating, but your commission check was short this month. You might ask if you could cook at home, or you might suggest a movie instead. Or, if your partner is running low on cash, you could offer to prepare a picnic for your next eating-out adventure. You might even pick up the restaurant tab, but be careful that you don't try to keep a partnership definition going all by yourself.

Defining from your partner's need takes away your ability to define from your Heart, which does away with your space. Having an empty space eliminates your ability to share. You may have filled your partner's space and temporarily solved his or her problem for the present; however, for the long term, you have created problems for your partner, yourself, and the relationship.

Emotional Spending

Money is a key energy exchange token. You put your energies into a job and you get money in exchange. Since you need money to survive, this job/money exchange can cross your thinking wires into believing that money also represents love or other things you feel you need in order to survive. When this happens, you will expect your partner to spend money on you for your needs to be met. You might even go so far as to say your partner doesn't love you unless she or he spends money on you.

This confusion around money also impacts the way you spend money on yourself. Some people "love" themselves by spending money on their cars or on their shoe fetish. Many, many people try to "nurture" themselves with chocolate or some other food treat. Still there are others who believe that "forgiveness" can be purchased. In all these examples, money serves as a cover-up for real Love.

While it is true that money is the foremost energy exchange token in society today, it is only just that — a token of exchange. It is not the needed energy. When you spend money hoping to meet a heart energy need, you are emotionally spending. If you take this pattern of emotional spending into your relationship, you might end up with lots of physical objects but very little substance.

While money cannot buy Friendship, Love, Appreciation, etc., it can be a carrier of those energies. For example, your partner might give you a beautiful piece of jewelry with the real intent of showing Love and Appreciation. Money, in this case, is a valuable token of exchange. However, just giving a beautiful piece of jewelry will mean nothing unless it is the carrier of good intent. The same object could be a gift of guilt, which nobody wants or needs.

Any and all purchases should start with the heart energy you want to receive, or in the case of a gift, share. Remember, anything short of this is an emotional purchase. Buying groceries for the family without the Heart's intent of Health is an emotional purchase. You are simply buying groceries because you feel you must have them, or you are hoping they will bring you Health. If you start with the energy of Health, then your money can be the connector between your energy and that of the food.

As you can see, money can be a powerful force for good in a relationship or it can be wasted. After working hard for your money, it is sad to waste it simply because you haven't been taught its real purpose. Wrongful spending is much like using a table knife as a screwdriver. It may get the screw to go in, but the knife will be wasted. You may get food, but Health will be wasted.

Beginning a relationship
from the place of needing someone
to fill in the blanks
is not an ideal starting place.

Dating

16

For you who are single reading this book, this is a perfect time to evaluate your position in the world of dating. You now have a better grasp on what a healthy relationship can look like as well as how to get there. The unanswered question is, "Do you want to be in a romantic relationship at this point in your life?" A good place to start is by checking to see if you are ready for relationship.

Are You Ready for Relationship?

While there are many questions to be answered that will help you in determining your readiness for a relationship, the most important one is, "Am I wanting someone to complete me?

In other words, are you wanting someone to make you happy, make you feel desirable, keep you from being lonely, or supply the money? If the answer to any of those is yes, then you need someone to complete a part of your life. Beginning a relationship from the place of needing someone to fill in the blanks is not an ideal starting place.

People usually hide their energetic neediness from others and themselves by saying they just want to love and be loved. And there is a trace of truth in that statement. However, the place to start in the love arena is not with another person, but with yourself. You can only love another person to the extent that you love yourself. Trying to find, rather than resonate, Love is a losing proposition. By acknowledging the Love you have within you, you actually start an energetic movement. The acknowledged Love will flow out and touch someone's energy field that has the same vibration. You will literally be pulled together in the physical from the power of your Hearts connecting energetically.

You cannot make someone more loving by giving more physical things. Even if, for example, you bring a lot of Love through physical gifts to someone who has not grown his or her Love energy, you will get back only as much as that person can receive. That person will receive only as much as she or he has within. Simply stated, you will resonate with the heart energy of Love to the lowest common denominator — yours or theirs. I am not saying you can't bring Love through physical gifts — you can. But you cannot force something to exist that doesn't.

The good news about sharing Love through resonating is that you get to empower each other's Love. While you must have the heart energy of Love to offer before you can receive any from others, you will never grow your Love to a bigger size until it gets to resonate with other people's Love. The desire to love someone so much that the person will just have to love you back is not a real truth about how Love works. However, the desire to love so that your Love can grow is the real truth.

This process of offering a heart energy to resonate with the other person's heart energy will also work with energies other than Love. When you can offer Love, Support, Play, Commitment, etc., from a full supply within yourself, then you are ready for a relationship. It is true that everyone has needs. However, it is not true that other people can meet those needs. All of your needs are heart energy based and are available within you. The feeling that something is missing in your life is your cue that your Heart wants to be acknowledged so that it can flow out and resonate. Once you start claiming those "need energies" within you, you will activate a magnetic charge in your energy field (aura) that will pull to you a resonating relationship instead of an empty one.

Just as real energy pulls to you real energy, so do empty patterns pull to you empty patterns. Let's say you have the pattern of giving in to others' wants and shutting your wants out of the picture. If this is your empty pattern, then you will draw to you people who want to have their way all the time. Thus, their empty pattern of taking rather than resonating, and your empty pattern of giving rather than resonating, get to play out. I refer to this type of pattern-matching as external balance. Only people who share real energy expression can have what I call resonance balance.

Without filling your need with realness first, you will create the exact opposite of what you want in a partner. You will create someone who helps you continue your empty patterns of thinking, feeling, or acting. Empty patterns equal unconscious neediness rather than need recognition. Therefore, entering a relationship on empty will only increase your emptiness. This, by the way, is the exact opposite of what you hope will happen.

After you have asked yourself what your biggest needs are and have looked inside to fill them, you can ask question number two, which is vitally important to your future, "How do I want to share the heart energies that I have claimed within myself?" There are as many ways to share who you are with another person as there are people. Deciding on how you want to share yourself with another gives your Heart instructions as to what shapes it will take in its expression and magnetic attraction.

For instance, let's imagine you have now claimed self-love and are ready to share Love with another person. First, you might try out some possible ways to share it with a few close friends. After picking and choosing from the many possible expressions of your Love, you can begin to write out your relationship list. You can state that you want a relationship partner who will share Love through two main forms. One could be staying at home and cuddling, and the other could be holding hands and kissing.

The reason for laying down some ground rules is that the magnetism of the Heart is so great that it will pull in all kinds of Love shapes if it isn't given proper direction. You will need to know what fits you best so you can pick and choose with accuracy. If you are a flexible person, then you can just ask for Love and define it with your partner when he or she comes along. You must know yourself well to know what best fits you.

A third and very important question that you will need to answer before you are ready for a relationship is "Which three heart energies are my favorites?" If you don't love or nurture yourself very well, then you need to keep those energies as personal development projects. Instead, you will want to ask for energies that you have in large measure. At least you will want to do that if you want a big relationship. Perhaps Play and Adventure are your biggest heart energies. Then they would be a much better choice than your small energies of Love and Nurturing. However, if you choose a relationship for its growth potential, then choosing a partner that matches your smaller heart energies so they can grow from resonating would be the better choice.

It is an unfortunate fact that people usually want from others what they don't want to give themselves. Don't fall into that common trap. It never works. Unfulfilled needs create empty patterns that only attract other empty patterns. Big heart energies attract big heart energies.

Learning from Past Experiences

The best way to discover who you are and who you aren't (yet) is through relationships. Those relationships don't have to be romantic ones to be good teachers. It is usually easier to see ourselves with clear perspective through others' broader perspectives than through our own limited sight. For example, you may have seen yourself as patient until you got into a relationship with someone who had ten times more Patience than you. The broader perspective of Patience made you aware beyond your previous limited sight. Or you may have thought you had little Compassion until you experienced someone with zero. Relationships put the size of your heart energies into perspective. You get to see through their eyes the things your eyes haven't seen before.

The minute you see yourself in a new light, everything else becomes the past. If you stand in judgment of your past experiences, then you get turned around and become stuck in the past. But if you can be honest about the size of energies you brought to your relationships in the past and the size needed now, you can begin to define with more accuracy. For instance, you could define ways to grow your lagging Patience, and also decrease your expectations of Compassion from those with less. On the other hand, you might decide to find new people with smaller sizes of Patience or bigger portions of Compassion in order to match the size needed in the present.

One of the greatest obstacles to learning from past experiences is attachment. As long as one piece of the relationship fits, you'll likely tolerate the other parts that don't fit. Even if the "non-fitters" aren't emotionally pleasing, you can become so attached to the one good heart energy expression that you will lump the "fit" and "non-fit" together and hold on tight. This attachment to what doesn't work can keep you from creating what does work. It also keeps you on hold and prevents you from fully stepping into the future. Attachment is the antithesis to growth in relationships.

In the early stages of dating someone, look to see if you are creating the same attachment behavior patterns that you had in the last relationship. In other words, are you hanging on to the one or two good traits and overlooking or making excuses for the bad ones? I have seen people repeat the same list of problems in as many as five different relationships. They would find someone who corrected the worst trait of the last relationship only to find new, and sometimes worse, traits. They never gave up their attachment to having only a few of their needs met.

The fear that you cannot have anything better than what you have right now is sure death. It is death not only to you individually, but to your relationship as well. This fear stems from believing that your heart energies are fixed and powerless. Unless you understand that you are your heart energies and that those parts of you have the capacity to grow and change, you will cling to whatever you have outside of you and believe the untruth that you can have nothing better. You are in control of your life! You are the creator of your Heart's desires.

How many people do you know who believe there is a whole section of potential partners out there that would have nothing to do with them? If you are one of those people, give up that untruth! You have any and all the choices in the world. However, all potentials may not fit your Heart's desires. Your Heart can and will create the exact person with whom you need to be in relationship. Social standing, looks, money, occupation, education, family background — none of these create or block your Heart from drawing to you the exact right person. You are the one who does the blocking by holding on to past patterns, people, or beliefs. Or you may block what your Heart wants to give you because you feel too unworthy. You may feel unworthy because of who you have been or because of who you haven't yet allowed yourself to become. It doesn't matter what is limiting your bigger vision of who you are and what you need right now; you can step beyond those limitations and chart a new course.

Charting a New Course

Drawing to you what you have claimed internally and having it appear in forms of your choosing is "a piece of cake" if you let go of all false images of who you are and how your life must be. This new awareness about yourself, and what is false, must also be carried over to the other person. The biggest glitch most people have in charting a new course is being taken in by the mirage in which others wrap themselves. Once caught up in this fantasy, they unknowingly think they have found "the real McCoy." It is usually much later they discover that it was all fake.

This mirage is energetically like a thick, gray cloud with no see-through visibility. People put on this false wrap when they want to be seen as more than they believe themselves to be.

Within the cloud, they will project images of what they perceive relationship perfection to look like. Keep in mind that these images are only illusions, but they appear to be the real thing. Some people have become quite accomplished at presenting a counterfeit image to a potential relationship partner. So beware.

With your present understanding of how relationships work, you know this false, pretentious presentation is not going to offer what you want. However, its effects can still dazzle a neophyte. In fact, some mirage presentations can even befuddle a veteran in search of a real match. So how do you avoid this pitfall in charting your new course? Rule #1 is to look through the eyes of your Heart, not your emotions. Rule #2 is to stand in your real energy space, not your empty patterns. Rule #3 is to see if the other person has any true resonance with the heart energies you have chosen to bring.

Following these three rules will get you past the charlatans and keep you walking down your defined path. Don't settle for less than you have to bring. You must also be willing to wait for your relationship energies to draw to you their perfect fit. While your energies will magnetically pull to you the perfect match, they may also pull in several possible fits before your vision gets completely refined. Don't stop looking until you know it is the right one.

Finding Mister or Miss Right

Most people want a life mate, but not all are ready for one. It may take several tries before you find someone who is willing to keep growing with you. As long as growth is your primary goal and relationship is a secondary one, you will escape the dead-end verdict of a stagnant life (and relationship). So Mister or Miss Right may be only temporary.

One lady I know had four right relationships before finding her life mate. The first relationship started with her valuing the partner's intelligence more than her own Wisdom. This relationship was about empty patterns. She brought the feelings, and he made all the decisions. Neither brought a balance of heart energies to the relationship. This didn't mean they weren't both heartful people, but they tried to create balance externally before claiming internal balance. This worked for awhile until she started yearning for Wisdom. Of course she didn't have the clarity to call it Wisdom, but her Heart started bringing it to her in the form of books and people.

Once she claimed Wisdom, she pulled to her a relationship that could share Wisdom. This felt truly wonderful at first, but after a few years a new part of herself was ready to emerge. Having found her inner Wisdom only enhanced her desire to express herself more passionately in the world. Passion began to grow within her. Of course that drew to her lots of people who attached Passion and sex together. That did throw her off balance for a time, but soon she refocused on her desire to embrace life passionately. When her energy of Passion got big enough to have a magnetic pull, she drew to herself a man whose Passion for life was inspiring, and for a few years this resonance was totally fulfilling.

Even though the relationship resonated with Passion, it grew no other heart energies. With Passion all grown up, Honesty began to clamor for attention. She began by being Honest with herself. Once this was mastered, she was ready to try out relationship Honesty. She was ready for the relationship to grow a new heart energy, but her partner was attached to how things had been and didn't want any change. So she left. Her next relationship creation was a man who not only was totally honest, but was able to allow her to be that also.

Now it appeared she had it all — Wisdom, Passion, Honesty. However, the only thing she needed that she hadn't created up to this point was a partner who would keep growing with her. Even though she was growing, she hadn't really seen the need for relationship Growth. As she outgrew each situation, she discarded her partners, believing she had chosen wrongly. She actually had chosen well for each new piece. She just hadn't defined the heart energy of Growth as a necessary quality for her partners to have. Once she figured out the missing piece of Growth, she was ready for a life mate. Had she opted for a permanent relationship before she grew Wisdom, Passion and Honesty, she might never have seen the need for Growth, and thus never made it to permanency.

Be careful not to label a relationship with Mr. Right or Miss Right until you have mastered the basics. The lady in the above story wanted each of her three "pre"-relationships to last, but she was able to see the signs and let go before the stench of death took over. Let the glow of early resonance have its day in the sun, but don't count on one main energy to pull you through a lifetime of togetherness. Gain as many heart energies as you need in order to realize that growth is an on-going business. There is always one more energy to be achieved when life is about growth. Creating a relationship that contains the energy of Growth means your partner can continue traveling life's journey with you.

When Can I Consider this a Permanent Relationship?

Beyond the growth factor, there are a few points to consider before making a relationship permanent. You won't be ready for a permanent relationship until you no longer need one. You must also be able to enjoy several facets of a relationship without attachment to one favorite part. Having favorite parts of a relationship usually means that you are attached to getting those energies from outside of yourself. This isn't to say that you can't have good things happening within your relationship. Why be there if you don't? However, needing good offerings from a partner and enjoying them are two different things.

When you can just enjoy the relationship and not need it to be there for your life to continue in a good way, you may then be ready to consider whether you want to spend the rest of your life with this person. While enjoyment without neediness is an important measure, you must add into that measuring the assurance that you are enjoying the resonance of shared heart energies rather than an attractive pattern. A person can act out one pattern with you and be another with someone else. Patterns vary from interaction to interaction. Heart energies don't. For example, if your prospective life mate has the energy of Support, she or he will be supportive in more areas of life than with just you — so look beyond the microcosm to the macrocosm. See how supportive your partner is of people outside the two of you. Then you can be sure that your enjoyment will last.

The kicker comes when you want your partner to be a certain way with you, and only with you — no one else. You may enjoy your companion's Generosity towards you, but be jealous of it being directed toward anyone else. If that Generosity can be limited to only you and your relationship, then it isn't a heart energy at all. Instead, it is only a nice pattern. Nice patterns wear out. When frustrations enter the picture, heart energies don't leave, but nice patterns do. You can't be selfish with the Heart.

Naturally, nice patterns are better than bad ones, but either way, they are empty, and empty doesn't have a lasting value. So don't decide whether relationships have permanent qualities until you have seen the other person in action in several situations outside of your relationship. Give them the space to share with others and appreciate who they are in the world. For instance, you can learn a lot just by listening to who they were in their last relationship. Don't be jealous if they were kind and loving there. Instead, know that you have hit real gold. On the other hand, if they have nothing of value to tell you about their "exes," then beware; you may be the next "ex."

Have you ever read any of your friends' profiles on the Internet dating sites? Some of them may be close to the truth, but many are a bit slanted. You can count on that persona to be carried out as much and as long as possible. Persona people believe the charade is better than their real self or they wouldn't have written it up as a dating profile. Who a person wants to be or thinks he or she should be provides a strong impetus for birthing empty patterns. You cannot be who you aren't for very long no matter how much you want to. A charade is a charade. No matter how pretty it looks, it is not real. The more real you are, the more you will be able to see real and detect the pretenders.

Being with an empty pattern person gets to be wearing after awhile. For instance, you may get tired around a well-acted-out empty pattern and not even understand what is happening. Empty patterns are like vampires — they suck up all available energy around them. They are empty holes. Acting from a persona, or being with someone who is acting from one, is like holding a cardboard person between you. Both of you will tire of it at some point, but not necessarily at the same time. So check your energy level after spending a lengthy period of time with your potential partner and see if you are energized or drained.

In summary, you can decide if your new relationship is a keeper when

- you have factored in Growth,
- you have gotten your need for a relationship under control,
- you register on the plus side of enjoyment blessings, you have become aware of the empty patterns, and
- you have experienced your prospective partner's realness beyond the two of you.

This list may seem a little overwhelming, but you have as much time as it takes.

Oh My, There are Flaws!

Even though you have found some real gems in this new person, you have also found some empty patterns. Now what? Let's start with the "do not" list.

1. Don't fixate on the flaws.
2. Don't ignore the flaws.
3. Don't assume you can lovingly erase the flaws.

So where does that leave you? You must put the flaws in perspective.

I knew a man who was kind and supportive, but he was afraid for anyone to see him as inadequate. This fear caused him always to have an answer for everything. This worked fine when there was a right answer needed. However, his girlfriend soon got sick and tired of constantly being corrected by "right answers." This empty pattern became her focus, and thus, in her perception, the flaws got way out of proportion to his Kindness or Support.

To keep empty patterns in perspective means you must handle them when they come up by recognizing them as nothing more than what they are — empty. If you treat them as real and powerful, you will find yourself exhausted from punching at the persona the other person is holding up. Also recognize that there is probably not a person alive who doesn't have some empty patterns. You just have to decide how many and which ones you can handle.

Regarding #3 on the list: While it is true that some fear-based flaws may ease or even disappear in a loving atmosphere, placing your bets on the future is gambling. Make your decision on the cards that are out on the table. Do not count on the ones you think might be hidden underneath.

Sometimes empty pattern flaws can be defined out of the shared space. For example, a friend of mine has an empty pattern of letting her emotional need to be the "served princess" keep her from doing her part of any shared task. Her boyfriend has wisely pushed that pattern out of the together space by dividing up the chores instead of sharing tasks. When they eat together, he defines that he will cook if she will clean up. They never cook and clean together. When she wants her feet rubbed, he agrees only if she will do his first. He is not being small and unkind, but wise. Her pattern allows for very little give-and-take because her heart energy of Balance has been pushed out by the princess syndrome.

Flaws in a person are normal, but that doesn't mean they should have a "normal" place in a relationship. See them for what they are and deal with them accordingly, but don't let the flaws get in the way of the good qualities. Keeping everything in perspective may mean doing something as basic as keeping a written list to remind you how many flaws and how many attributes your partner has to offer. It also helps to keep a journal about how much you have enjoyed the good experiences so you can go back and remember, when your anger tries to erase all good memories.

Make sure you don't label differences as flaws. Two people can have the exact same heart energy and express it in opposite patterns. This doesn't make either pattern empty — just different. One person may express Sharing by talking about what happens and how he or she feels about it, while another may express Sharing by giving things to people. Obviously, neither of these expressions is a flaw, but it may be seen that way to the two opposite sharers unless they look inside the pattern to see the real intent.

Should I Cut My Losses and Leave?

Before you make a decision on whether to stay in a relationship or leave it, you need to have a clear picture in your mind about which of your heart energies you most enjoy sharing with a person on a regular basis. If those energies are presently being shared, then you need to start the inventory

I talked about earlier in this chapter. If not, then you should probably just cut your losses and leave.

If you are pretty sure your relationship is not going to be "the one," but is filling a valuable space right now, pace yourself. Pacing simply means that you don't need to pour all that you have into it. Even if it were possible to resonate together with three small energies and one big one, you may want to limit your involvement if those energies aren't the primary ones you want to share. Putting all you have to offer into a temporary thing is no different from spending lots of money on decorating a house you plan to live in for only a few months. Instead, see what is offered in this newly defined, temporary relationship, and focus on that as a part-time offering. A part-time offering means part-time hours. Spending lots of time and energy on a temporary relationship is a foolish investment that will shrink your space.

It is important that you spend time in places that give equal return. In other words, you would not want to spend every night with someone who offers only two of your fifteen big heart energies. So the "cut and leave" theory may apply to cutting back on time instead of cutting yourself out of the relationship altogether. Obviously, you need a small dose of what is available, or your Heart wouldn't be offering it to you. Just be careful not to give more than the space can hold. Do not hang on to the giver past the gift's usefulness.

People often throw themselves into a relationship before they have even evaluated what is there and what fits. They close the door to their other friendships and start shrinking those previously expressed parts of themselves in order to fit the new and exciting possibility of a relationship. Note I said possibility — not reality. Be careful to not throw away the known for the unknown. However, you must be equally careful not to hang on to the known for fear of the unknown.

Instead of throwing out your old friendships when a new relationship comes along, re-evaluate who you are and what outlets for expression each relationship provides. Then you will have a basis to know which ones you should cut away. Only by re-evaluating how many and what expression outlets you need at a particular time will you be able to budget both your time and energy. Said another way, what are your energy needs at this point in time, and where can you best meet those needs? What you need at any point is to express all of who you are. Since you can't know who you are going to be in the future, the only other energy that must be added to your list is Growth. Once Growth is included on the "who-you-are list," it should hold a position of top priority in your evaluation process. I highly encourage you to cut your losses and leave if Growth is not part of the relationship you are considering for long term. A perfect match for now won't be perfect in the future if Growth is not in the mix.

Okay I'm Staying. Now What?

Once you decide your relationship has future potential, your first instinct probably will be to start pressuring your partner into making the same choice. While pushing is not a good idea, in that it will chase most people away, it is important to know where the other person stands on the subject of commitment. Find out what his or her track record has been and measure that against what is now being said.

When people share about past relationships, they usually glamorize their personal role in the bad experiences. Take the glamour out by recognizing that every interaction requires more than one participant. It takes two people to fight. It takes two people to distance from each other. And even if one partner is unfaithful, there are two sides to that story also. Imagine yourself being your partner's ex and decide how you would have responded to the same circumstance. Don't look at how you would have responded after the blow-up, but instead look at how you would have played the other person's role before the blow-up.

If both of you have decided this relationship has future potential, you can then start making plans for the future together. You may both want to impose your image of a future together on the relationship. Don't go there. Instead, start by painting two separate pictures. Put them side by side and see which portions fit together, which ones overlap and which ones need to be separated. This is an important step in answering the "now what" part of the, "I'm staying, so now what" question.

While it is true that no one, not even good psychics, can predict all changes of the future, you can certainly project from where you are in the now. However, you must be careful not to project from what you emotionally want, but instead project from who you are as energies of the Heart. For instance, you may emotionally want to have someone rave about your talents and tell you repeatedly how great you look. You can ask for those emotional feel-good gifts and enjoy them, but don't base your future on them. They cannot be projected into the future even if they are important to you now because feel-goods are momentary things. What feels great this year may get old and seem hollow next year. Emotional needs are ego-based and temporary. They have no lasting value. Energy needs are Heart-based and permanent. Even though energy is constantly moving and changing, it doesn't evaporate. It evolves into bigger, brighter shapes.

Internet Dating

While Internet dating is not the answer for everyone, it is a solution for those who don't have a way to meet people easily. Location, limited free time and shyness are probably the main factors that encourage people to meet on the Internet. Of course everyone's profile presents the person in the best possible light, but is that really any different from talking to someone in physical meeting places? If the truth be told, you have to always dig beneath the surface to discover the true essence of just about everyone. Few people are brave or honest enough to put themselves out on public display.

Internet meeting rules are not any different from in-person meeting rules. You have to know who you are to know what you are looking for in another person. You have to be able to see below the surface, and not be taken in by charm and good looks. Remember, ego attraction isn't a lasting factor. This doesn't mean you can't add sexual chemistry to your list of highly desired qualities to have. Of course you can and you should, but you can't build a relationship on physical attraction alone (even though many people try).

As with all first dates, plan a meeting away from your home in a public place, and let a friend know where you are and who you are with. For safety, check in with your friend at the end of the evening. After all, people with a criminal intent can put on a friendly face, too. It is better to be safe than sorry.

If sex comes up on the agenda, have blood tests done first. Some of you are groaning that all the excitement and spontaneity of dating is quickly fading from the dating scene with all these security measures crowding into the mix. Risk and spontaneity are not one and the same. Planned safety doesn't take away anything that is real and lasting. It is much better to wait a while for reckless abandonment until you know who you are with and how they fit into your relationship world.

While first impressions do have an impact, presenting a false image to make a good first impression implies that you don't feel as if all parts of you are relationship material. In fact, some people turn to Internet dating simply because they believe they can create a better mirage on paper than in real life. The hope behind this lie is that once you "catch" someone, the person will be willing to tolerate your faults. It is the whole mix of realness — with all your faults and virtues combined — that makes an interesting package. Who would want to date a perfect robot? No one would. It takes the shadowed areas as well as the light ones to give a picture contrast and depth.

Dating, either by Internet or in-person, is all about the unfolding of two people with each other. Strengths and weaknesses need to be revealed as they come up. They should neither be pushed forward nor held back. You are a package of big and little heart energies expressed through a variety of patterns; so are others. The patterns don't have to be graceful and charming, just filled with realness. The only things you need to watch out for are the empty patterns. While everyone has a few of the empty kind, they should be eliminated from the relationship space as soon as possible. If an unreal expression (better known as their well-rehearsed lines) pops its ugly head into the conversation, all you have to do is ignore it as unimportant. Anything dies without food, even empty words.

Eliminating pretentious and manipulative patterns at the onset of a relationship will save a lot of upset later on. One easy way to discern what is real and what isn't is by digging beneath the surface of all statements. Check to see if what was said in a previous conversation fits with the present one. Ask questions. Be aware that flattery usually wants something in return. You don't have to be a cynic to make sure you are not being swooped up in a swirl of hot air.

If you can express yourself better in writing than in words, the Internet is a great place for you. Go for it. But let me throw in a word of warning. Don't forget to express your feelings when writing. Since school has trained people to put only their thoughts on paper, the tendency is to leave the feelings out when meeting someone on the Internet. This will not give you a true picture of the relationship. Remember it is the necessary contrast of shading in a picture that makes it three-dimensional, so don't leave out either the negative or positive feelings.

A tool for learning to express feelings through your writing is journal keeping. Opening up to this feeling element within yourself will open the door for more of you to come out in the relationship unfolding process. In addition to enriching your relationships, becoming aware of your feelings will also help you to bring more of you to your everyday activities. Life can flat line without the passion and zeal that honest emotions bring.

I'm not sure why people find the sharing of feelings to be so scary at first. Those same scared people will share all the gory details of a movie they have seen, be honest about their choice of books and movies, and openly admit they don't like the way you make coffee. So why is it so hard to throw in a feeling? It is probably because, if you discount physical abuse, feelings are the main doorway to hurt. It is this "doorway-to-hurt" belief that has created the inner voice that whispers from your unconscious, "Don't share any feelings; they will make you too vulnerable."

While no one likes to be hurt or feel vulnerable, the alternative is not better. The alternative is a flat, two-dimensional life with secretive, dishonest relationships. So start with the basics. Be aware and honest about what you are feeling first with yourself, and then bring it to your relationship. Admit your feelings of weakness, not as an invitation for hurt, but for ownership. Let it be okay to be vulnerable and less than perfect. There will always be enough competent parts of you to bring balance.

Owning your emotions means that you are ready to claim responsibility for your shortcomings as well as your gifts. This is a very important step in becoming a real grown-up instead of opening a door to hurt, as emotional sharing without ownership can do. Emotional owning will liberate you, once you admit there is a part of you that needs help. Then and only then can you have help, either personally or from the support of someone else.

Another side of ownership is admitting you have valuable gifts to share. Before you can fully share any part of yourself, you must own it. Don't be afraid to state your strengths. Saying you are strong in a particular area isn't bragging when you are presenting the whole package of who you are. It is just one more piece.

This brings us to another valuable use of internet dating — getting to know yourself better. If your goal is to snare a partner by hook or by crook, you probably will do just that. However, if your goal is to get acquainted with yourself by owning all that you share with another person, then you will have used your dating service in a valuable way.

By changing your approach to relationship,
you can change your approach
to all areas of your life.

Beginnings and Endings

17

The Right Start

If you are planning a marriage, or if you are thinking of renewing your vows, please consider a tailored fit. While the traditions around marriage have many good features, they don't work for everyone. The right start is imperative for charting a good course. It means that you have outlined every step of a course that will support the two of you in creating the best third entity relationship that the two of you are capable of birthing.

Tradition has deeply rooted concepts about what steps should be taken by a couple who wish to marry. The "normal" traditional marriage begins by having a wedding conducted by a minister, priest, rabbi or justice of the peace. This ceremony is followed by a honeymoon of some sort in which the couple celebrates the love they have discovered. The couple then moves in together and begins the task of joining their lifestyles and their bank accounts. The possibility of children, pets and/or relatives playing some role in their joined lives is discussed. After all these big items are settled, generally the pressures of life are then allowed to creep back into their reality, and the maintenance part of marriage begins.

While this description may not have nailed the construction of your marriage in totality, it probably did hit some of the pieces. While some, or even most, of the pieces may have been the perfect fit, there might have been a few other possibilities that would have worked better.

Let's start with the location of the ceremony. If the intent is only to be legal, then just about any location works. However, if the intent is to find the most sacred setting either of you has ever experienced, the norm may or may not work. Perhaps the most sacred setting for you may be by the ocean or in the woods. While most churches and temples are defined to be sacred places, it doesn't mean that all individuals feel their Sacredness. For instance, if you were forced to go to church as a child by a parent who came home and treated you badly, then church may not feel sacred to you. On the other hand, you may have created a place of Safety, Comfort and Sacredness in your own home or apartment. You can have both legality and Sacredness, so don't shortchange yourself.

The ceremony itself has been pretty much the property of each religious denomination. That ceremony may describe exactly the heart energies the two of you have joined, but then again it may not. Of course you will want to look nice and have your friends celebrate with you, but more importantly, you will want the service to be a foundation to lock in place, through sacred ceremony, the heart of your relationship.

It is important that the people you invite be carriers of at least one of the heart energies that you have chosen to be a binding force in your relationship. They also need to understand that they are more than observers of a beautiful wedding. They are there to covenant together with the two of you that this marriage will be honored by all present — now and in the future. They must bring a gift of the Heart that either matches or supports the heart energies that are defining your relationship, or they will not be able to support you through resonance.

The honeymoon is traditionally seen as a time when both of you are to reach a pinnacle of romance and love never before experienced by either. That is a tough order to fill and puts a lot of pressure on one or both of you. Wouldn't it make more sense to either wait until you both needed a change of scenery, or use that time simply to try out the heart energies you have defined around your marriage? Giving up the traditional expectation that you will experience more Passion than you have up to this point not only releases the pressure, but it allows you to celebrate each other and the relationship in a relaxed way.

However or whenever you take your honeymoon, it should be for the purpose of strengthening what you already have, not for trying to take you several steps beyond where you are at that time. Looking at the honeymoon from that perspective may change where you go, where you stay, and even how long you stay.

One couple I know turned down an offer to honeymoon in Europe and instead spent a week driving and camping in the North Carolina Mountains. They were weak in the talking kind of Communication, but were strong in communicating with nature. The honeymoon gave them the opportunity to resonate Communication from where they were so that it could grow into something bigger.

Joining lifestyles, even similar ones, is a monumental task. Even if the joining is seen as sharing instead of doing everything together, some ingenuity is required. Instead of feeling the need to do it all at once, give yourself the freedom to do it one piece at a time.

For a physically active person to give up sports or try to drag along a partner who doesn't enjoy them at all is not only unfair but unhealthy. The list of differences in lifestyles goes on and on. One may spend lots of time meditating. Another person may express through a creative outlet like pottery or woodworking. Whatever the differences may be, they need to be acknowledged, and a simple, uncomplicated joining point needs to be found.

Most areas of expression have places that can be shared without requiring total involvement from the other person. Sharing your life is not the same as doing everything the same. The sports person could come home and share his or her Enthusiasm for the game. The meditating person could offer some of the Peace and Contentment experienced through meditation simply by listening from that state when the partner is agitated. The person with Creativity might share money made from selling his or her works of art. Keep in mind that joining lifestyles through a point of sharing still requires total involvement of both people at that time.

Giving your marriage the right start is vitally important to the ongoing well-being of your relationship. Be willing to step away from the accumulated traditions, and tailor-fit your wedding, honeymoon, and joining of lifestyles to the two of you. You have a unique relationship unlike any other in the whole world. By upholding your uniqueness as special, you can withstand the pressures to follow the norm of family, friends and even your church.

Closure

The need for closure appears many times in a relationship. At the ending of each definition, an inventory needs to be taken to see how a single heart energy, or group of energies, has manifested in the third entity relationship space. It is also necessary to see how your individual lives have been impacted by those energies. It is only through closure that you can initiate new spaces.

Once you take inventory and see how all three spaces (yours, theirs and ours) have been blessed, you may be tempted to keep defining the same energies over and over. As you can imagine, continually hanging on to the "same-ole, same-ole" eliminates both Growth and Spontaneity from happening. It is by viewing closure as both necessary and desirable that a relationship can birth new and vibrant heart energies.

Closure also needs to happen when a new phase of living becomes necessary. A new phase may be brought on by someone new coming to live in your house, or it might occur at an ending — such as a loss of a job or a relocating. Any time a shift is made in your living situation, the old needs to be both celebrated and grieved. It is only through doing both sides of closure — the celebration and the grieving — that an accurate inventory can be made as to which energies need to stay, which need to be eliminated, and which need to be birthed. Of course, redefining must take place and new patterns of thinking, feeling and acting must be practiced at the conclusion of each celebration/grieving closure.

Sometimes the new situation looks so good that it is hard to grieve the old, while on the other hand, you may be so caught in grief that you forget to celebrate the good that came from that phase of your life. I never will forget when my grandmother died what a difficult time I had in getting beyond my grief to celebrate all the heart energies we shared. However, had I not gotten to the celebration, that phase of my life would have remained open only to the loss with no space for anything new to come in.

Redefining your relationship space may mean ending the marriage and becoming friends. Or it may need to go so far as to define only an acquaintance relationship. Some marriages have such dysfunctional closure that all the good is no longer available and all that can be defined is separate parenting to the children. Even if the closure contract determines that you will never see or speak to each other again, the relationship will not have been a waste if you salvage, by claiming as heart gifts, all that was good. Whatever your co-agreement happens to be, there needs to be closure by releasing the bad and owning the good.

In situations that were originated with a ceremony, it is good to end them with one also. For example, if you had a wedding ceremony to begin your marriage, it would be fitting to complete your marriage with a divorce ceremony. Closure ceremony is also a good tool in completing with pets, cars, houses, etc. Perhaps you poured champagne over your new car to christen it. While you probably would not choose to do the champagne thing again, you might write down all the heart energies the car helped you express, and then burn the paper in ceremonial fashion. All endings need closure for new beginnings to be given a full life.

Every person and object in your life is there to provide you with an opportunity to express who you are — your Heart. When that expression happens repeatedly during a phase of a relationship or during the life of an object, then enough energy gets generated for that phase to have an identity. You wouldn't think of leaving a dead body lying around. Yet "energy entities" are often left lying around.

Closure doesn't mean losing all memories or good feelings about your past. It simply means that you have finished a chapter. All guilt, grief, Joy, Adventure, etc. gets to be acknowledged and then put to rest. How sad it is to see a college football star riding on those moments of past glory for the rest of his life. He can't go on to new present glories that are alive with the moment because the space is taken up with the old, nor can he fully receive the gift that the college phase of his life offered until he has found closure.

Closure is a time of receiving all that a phase of living offered. That includes the joy and the pleasure, as well as the sorrow and the pain. Having received all the obvious and hidden gifts, then it is time to close the book on that chapter. You are then able to engage fully in the next phase. The next phase may incorporate many of the same heart energies that the last one had, but with a different mix.

Up to this point we have looked at finding closure around two big situations, redefining the relationship space and ending a situational phase. Now let's look at the everyday closures that are just as important, even though they are smaller. This could be as simple as finding closure after you have gone to the grocery store. When you put your groceries away you can appreciate all the Health and Vitality that the food brings, and at the same time you can breathe out and release all the tension and frustration that was generated by dealing with unpleasant and non-caring people while at the store.

It is true that there isn't a whole lot of energy build-up around just going to the store. However, there should be a finished, clean space when you return, to prepare you for your next "adventure." Just before you get out of the car you might breathe out all your road rage and then take a few minutes to assess what your next "undertaking" will be. You are then ready to enter your house and express, without leaving behind any unclaimed gifts or clutter.

The time involved in getting closure is small compared to the benefits. You will actually be able to receive all that life has to offer — from the small to the large offerings. Think back to the grocery store situation. How often do you energetically receive anything from buying your groceries? Most people will answer never. A few will say sometimes, and an even smaller number will say always.

Once closure has become an everyday part of your life, you will become much more agile when it comes to ending chapters in your relationship book. Everyday closures also enable you to stay clear and responsive to your partner. You will truly be able to listen to and resonate with your partner, instead of thinking about that idiot who almost ran into your car when you were coming home from the store.

End of the day closure for couples is not only good for sleeping, but it is excellent for maintaining a Love space in your relationship. Taking a few minutes to talk together before you fall asleep or just writing a synopsis of the day in your couple's journal prepares you for a new beginning the next day. End of the day closure isn't about saying how many papers you signed or how many dishes you washed. Instead, it is for the purpose of identifying the ways your Heart expressed and making sure there are no judgments or upsets left hanging around to carry over into the next day.

Where Are You Now?

Whether you are looking for a relationship, beginning one, renewing one, or ending one, you need to take stock to see who you are and what you are willing to bring. All too often there is more attention given to what you want rather than who you are. This doesn't mean you can't have a say in what the other person brings to you. You certainly can. But focus brought to who you are magnetizes that energy, and pulls to you exactly what and who you need energetically. You then get to work in partnership to choose and define forms that work for both of you.

Ask yourself if you are willing and courageous enough to step into this new paradigm of relationship where heart energies are the subject. If you are, then you will need to do closure on past experiences and patterns so you can have a brand new start. By changing your approach to relationship, you can change your approach to all areas of your life. You will become more, work will become more, your relationships will become more, and your children will benefit in unbelievable ways. You can literally turn every area of your life into a Soulmate relationship.

Heart ENERGIES*

Abundance
Acceptance
Adventure
Affection
Awareness
Balance
Beauty
Birth
Brotherhood
Celebration
Clarity
Cleansing
Comfort
Commitment
Communication
Community
Compassion
Completion
Connection
Continuity
Courage
Creativity
Dedication
Delight
Determination
Devotion
Education
Efficiency
Endurance
Enthusiam

Expectancy
Faith
Flexibility
Flow
Focus
Forgiveness
Freedom
Gentleness
Grace
Gratitude
Growth
Harmony
Healing
Health
Honesty
Honor
Humility
Humor
Inspiration
Joy
Kindness
Light
Love
Loyalty
Mission
Nurturing
Obedience
Oneness
Openness
Order

Organization
Partnership
Passion
Patience
Peace
Persistence
Play
Power
Purification
Purpose
Relaxation
Release
Responsibility
Sacredness
Sharing
Simplicity
Spontaneity
Strength
Support
Surrender
Synergy
Synthesis
Tenderness
Transformation
Trust
Truth
Understanding
Unity
Willingness
Wisdom

*Heart energies are capitalized throughout the book.

About the Author

Jackie Woods was born with an extraordinary intuitive gift that has allowed her to be the recipient of angelic guidance. Acting from this angelic connection, Jackie has, through her teaching, lecturing, and writing, become a leading light in the movement to transform traditional healing. Her approach takes the emphasis off simply fixing the symptoms of life's everyday problems and supports people as they move beyond their old, unhealthy patterns of living. She does this by growing the complete Spirit of a person - which has become her mission and is summed up in her now-famous catch phrase, **"empowering your Heart for extraordinary living."**

Jackie is the author of two previous books, *Journey to Ultimate Spirituality* and *Spiritual Energy Cycles*, along with numerous audio recordings available on Compact Disc. She is also a frequent guest on nationally syndicated radio.

Jackie grew up in southern Missouri and after moving to Atlanta, Georgia, built a highly successful practice as a healer and teacher that lasted for over 20 years. In 1998, her intuitive guidance directed her to leave her individual practice and move to the foothills of the Blue Ridge Mountains where she founded **Adawehi** (Ah-dah-way-hee) **Institute, Healing School and Wellness Center**. Along with her loving husband and extended family, Jackie now lives and works on the 100-acre Adawehi campus. Adawehi supports her teaching mission by offering many forms of complementary healing as well as her Awareness Courses, both onsite and via the Internet. She invites you to visit her website, www.**jackiewoods.org** for more information.